IN THE BEGINNING, THE SUN

IN THE BEGINNING,

THE SUN

The Dakota Legend
of Creation

CHARLES ALEXANDER EASTMAN
(OHIYESA)

Edited by Gail Johnsen
and Sydney D. Beane

MINNESOTA
HISTORICAL
SOCIETY PRESS

COVER

Charles Alexander Eastman, riding; digital color by Hinhan Loud-hawk. The Dakota word for horse is sunka wakan, holy/mysterious dog. Members of the Horse Nation are spiritual beings and relatives to the Dakota people, teaching and helping through ceremonies, spiritual rides, and programs that carry traditional values to youth.

All photographs are from family collections.
Artwork on title and part title pages is by Yvonne Wynde.

mnhspress.org

The Minnesota Historical Society Press is a member of the Association of University Presses.

Manufactured in the United States of America

10 9 8 7 6 5 4 3 2 1

♾ The paper used in this publication meets the minimum requirements of the American National Standard for Information Sciences— Permanence for Printed Library Materials, ANSI Z39.48-1984.

International Standard Book Number
ISBN: 978-1-68134-233-7 (paperback)
ISBN: 978-1-68134-245-0 (e-book)

Library of Congress Control Number: 2022950119

This and other Minnesota Historical Society Press books are available from popular e-book vendors.

CONTENTS

PART 1
FAMILY ORIGINS

Charles Alexander Eastman, his son Ohiyesa,
and an unidentified friend (left to right).

A Journey through Time and Family

GAIL JOHNSEN

I OFTEN THINK OF THINGS I WISH I HAD ASKED MY MOTHER, my father, my grandparents. What were their early lives like? Why did they make the choices they did? What was most important to them? What made them who they were? Who were they, really? I will never know the answers to most of those questions, though there are hints in things they said or things they left.

That is probably why I accepted the papers and memorabilia left to my mother by her mother, Eleanor Mensel. These were things she had inherited in turn through her sister Dora, from their mother, Elaine Goodale Eastman, wife of Charles Alexander Eastman, whose Dakota name was Ohiyesa. I remember Elaine Eastman, and as I grew up, I knew three of Charles and Elaine's children: my grandmother, Eleanor, and her sisters Dora and Virginia. Charles himself had died before I was born.

Elaine Goodale Eastman, born in 1863, was an author throughout her life and also became an educator and an advocate

3

for Native people. In 1890, at the time of the Wounded Knee Massacre, she met Charles Eastman, a Dakota doctor working at the Pine Ridge Reservation in South Dakota, and she subsequently married him, to the consternation of some in her family. There was also a range of reactions in the press, with a number of articles romanticizing the union, some reporting it matter-of-factly, and a few decrying it.[1]

Charles Alexander Eastman was born in Minnesota in 1858; his mother did not survive his birth, and his grandmother raised him. It was a tumultuous time in Dakota history, the decade in which the bands were forced to move to a reservation as white settlers invaded their homelands. The government expected them to become farmers and to adopt the dress and customs of those who had taken their land; some people gave this a try, while others continued traditional lifeways. In 1862, when the US government failed to pay the promised annuities and Dakota children were starving, some of the Dakota attacked white settlements, beginning the US–Dakota War. Charles's grandmother fled with him to Canada, where he was adopted by his uncle, as his father was believed to be dead. He grew up in the Dakota way of life, and he was taught to consider the whites of the United States his enemies—until he was fifteen, when his world changed forever.[2]

Imagine the double shock of learning that his father was alive and had come to take him to Flandreau, South Dakota, to set him on a path to education and acculturation in the American society of the time. Only respect for his father enabled him to accede to the plan. It would mean not only learning a new language and new skills, but learning about a new religion and a new way of being in the world.

Charles went on to become a physician, government investigator, prominent advocate for Native Americans, lecturer, and author. In some areas of his life, he confronted prejudice in its various forms. Yet in his writing career, this seems not to have been as much of a factor. Early in the twentieth century, the United States saw a surge in general interest in nature, outdoor activities, and conservation—and, now that the Indian wars were essentially over, a more romantic view of the hundreds of Indigenous nations. These factors awakened interest in Native lore and skills. Charles both benefited from this interest and contributed to it. He wrote numerous books about Dakota life and beliefs with the collaboration of his wife. Her letters confirm that she considered him truly the author of the books, with her contribution in most cases being editing while preserving his style and voice.[3]

One of Eastman's goals in publishing books was to familiarize white America with a specific Native culture so that the dominant society might appreciate what the other had to offer. *Indian Boyhood* describes the childhood and training he had himself experienced. *Wigwam Evenings* sets out moral teachings in the context of traditional stories. Perhaps the most enduring of the books has been *The Soul of the Indian*, which outlines the values and spirituality of the society in which Charles Eastman had been raised as a child. In the foreword to *From the Deep Woods to Civilization*, Elaine Eastman stated that "in the end [he had] a partial reaction in favor of the earlier, the simpler, perhaps the more spiritual philosophy" of his Dakota upbringing.[4] This philosophy sprang from the teachings he referred to as the Unwritten Scriptures, summarized in Chapter 5 of *The Soul of the Indian*.

What if there were some further indication of his philosophy, his thoughts, in the papers that had been saved and passed down? Charles Eastman died in 1939 and left his papers to his wife, and I now had them. To go through and organize everything seemed like a daunting task, one that would require a lot of time and thought. So they sat for a while. I remembered that my grandmother Eleanor had said that various people had visited her, wanting to know more about her parents and hoping to gain access to any papers she had. She had demurred, telling them—and me—that she hoped someone in the family could do something with them. She expressed this desire in a letter to one researcher as well.[5]

After a time, I began to investigate those cartons of history. There were letters, photographs, pamphlets, papers, manuscripts, and books. There was categorizing to do, decisions about what and how much to keep, and what to do with the things kept.

Though there are no original manuscript drafts of Eastman's published works among the papers, the Eastmans kept manuscripts for some unpublished works. One thing that stood out was an old typed manuscript in a cover cut from cardboard, with a title page reading "Sioux Mythology / The Indians' Bible / The Story of the Creation / by Charles Alexander Eastman (Ohiyesa)." Eastman signed the last page, and there are a few handwritten notations made by his eldest daughter, Dora. This could be a more complete explication of the themes found in *The Soul of the Indian*.

I had also inherited a manuscript my mother received from a researcher who speculated that Elaine had donated Charles's unfinished works to a museum in South Dakota that had then suffered a fire, perhaps destroying both the writings and the record of them.[6] But my old typescript seemed to be that fuller exposition, and I searched for confirmation. In a 1935 letter to H. M. Hitchcock, a Minneapolis optometrist and amateur historian, Eastman claimed to have finished this work: "I have finally completed The Sioux Creation Legend. I called it [the] Sioux Bible. But I have to go over it again."[7]

Why did he work on this particular material at that point in his life? One factor might be the circular the new US commissioner of Indian Affairs, John Collier, had put out in 1934. It stated, "No interference with Indian religious life or ceremonial expression will hereafter be tolerated. The cultural liberty of Indians is in all respects to be considered equal to that of any non-Indian group." Until that time, the Code of Indian Offenses of 1883 had criminalized Native religious expression and much of the culture in general. Congress had also created Courts of Indian Offenses, which handed down harsh penalties for whatever actions they deemed to be infractions. The circular surely did not immediately wipe out all abuses—US laws made various Native religious practices illegal even after the passage of the American Indian Religious Freedom Act in 1978—but it was a significant change in policy and may have provided an impetus to Charles's work.

Elaine herself wrote that in Charles's later years, she and their son Ohiyesa felt that he had difficulty organizing his writing well.[8] The typescript I found may or may not represent collaboration with someone else. It is extremely doubtful that it was Elaine or another editor, particularly given the minor punctuation problems, very occasional typographical errors, indefinite pronoun references, and other small problems that editors correct automatically. We have made these minor revisions in this book, knowing that as a seasoned author, Charles would have welcomed this kind of editing. (For more details, see "A Note on Editing the Dakota Legend of Creation," page 193.) This is Charles Eastman's work, based on his memory of his early learning and, as he related, confirmed by a tribal elder and teacher.

So why did Elaine not try to publish this manuscript after Charles's death, especially considering that his other works had sold robustly, and she needed the income? She edited and published other pieces of his work, and she did not destroy or donate this manuscript. Looking at their later lives, it seems that both Charles and Elaine, with differing views, became more involved in advocating for the current status of Native Americans in American society, rather than in presenting a picture of a Dakota culture that could no longer be experienced. So it may be that since this manuscript represented what Elaine considered a reversion to a "simpler" philosophy, it went against her more assimilationist viewpoint. Also, the legends were of course stories, not a presentation of a more codified or even doctrinaire religion such as her own might seem. Further, as the manuscript expounded a philosophy of connectedness and community, it would not necessarily have resonated with a more individualistic and success-oriented cultural viewpoint. Finally, although she did publish "Peace Pipe and War Bonnet," an edited series of newspaper articles based on some of Charles's descriptions of the Dakota as they had been, she was unsuccessful in turning these into a published book and may have perceived that the timing for this sort of work was not right.

In his introduction to this manuscript, Eastman mentioned that he learned the legends as a child and first wrote them down in 1885, while he was a student at Dartmouth. He later consulted with his elder brother, John, to find out who still could repeat the entire cycle, in order to confirm his work. They went to an elder named Weyuha, who verified the main story and then repeated the twelve lessons of the legends that are given in this book. Echoing this process, as a descendant of Charles Eastman, I shared this manuscript with my cousin Syd Beane, a descendant of John Eastman, who consulted with tribal elders in an effort to verify the historicity of the teaching method. So this creation story, one story among many, traces back to an earlier time and culture, yet reverberates in the present day.

I began in hopes that the manuscript I found would tell me more about my great-grandfather, his values and their formation. In thinking about how we consider and frame his work and what we read into it, I realized we can also learn more about ourselves, our own prejudices or predispositions, our beliefs and values. And that's a good thing too. Hecetu ye. It is so.

John Eastman.

To Bend in the River and Beyond

SYDNEY D. BEANE

MY BROTHER WILLIAM AND I ARE NOW THE OLDEST LIVING direct descendants of John Eastman. We were both born and raised within the Bend in the River Dakota community as enrolled members of the Flandreau Santee Sioux Tribe. This is the Dakota community where Charles Alexander Eastman was baptized as a Christian and learned how to speak, read, and write in English while attending a mission school. Grandma Grace Moore, a daughter of Rev. John Eastman and Mary Jane Faribault Eastman, was our instructor in the family history and the books of her uncle Charles Eastman. She encouraged us to continue learning our family stories and to share them with others, and we do that here.

Coming to Bend in the River

In February of 1869 twenty-five Dakota families, mostly Bdewakantunwan who were originally from Cloud Man Village in Minnesota, left the Santee Reservation in Nebraska, crossed the Missouri River into South Dakota, and settled along the Big Sioux River at a place they called Wakpaipaksan—a Dakota word meaning "bend in the river." Their departure from Santee was a serious test of federal Indian policy. It was the Indian agent's responsibility to keep them on the reservation, but an 1868 treaty gave male Indians the right to claim homesteads in the Great Sioux Reservation. Their departure could be described as either a heroic act or a foolish decision, depending on one's point of view. Indians were still being killed outside their reservations.

The Big Sioux River Valley was a desirable area, and land development companies had competed for land claims and future townsites. One of them, the Dakota Land Company, was incorporated on May 21, 1857, during a session of the Minnesota territorial legislature. Legislation was further passed to create and name counties in what would become southwestern Minnesota and adjacent areas near the Big Sioux River. The Dakota Land Company claimed the site that would become the city of Flandreau, naming it in honor of Charles Flandrau, an associate supreme court justice for the Minnesota Territory and a Dakota Land Company shareholder. This townsite was abandoned within a year under pressure from the Yankton Sioux guardians of the nearby pipestone quarry. In 1862 Bdewakantunwan Dakota warriors led by Little Crow, furious and desperate over abuses of treaty provisions, went to war, and whites fled from the area. The city of Flandreau—spelled with the extra *e*—was officially established in 1879 after both white settlers and Dakota homesteaders occupied the valley.

The Flandreau area with its rolling hills and valleys along a major river became the place where Jacob Eastman (Many Lightnings, Wakandiota) established our family home following

the Dakota–US War of 1862. Jacob's family and kinship relations, although being on both sides of the war, experienced
hanging, exile, imprisonment, Christian conversion, and reservation life away from our homeland in Minnesota.

Jacob had become separated from his son Charles Alexander Eastman (Ohiyesa) after they fled Minnesota into Canada
during the war. After two years struggling to survive in Canada
with other kinship followers of Little Crow, Jacob, his daughter
Mary, and two of his sons, John and David, surrendered across
the Canadian border at Pembina. They were taken from Pembina and placed in the stockade at Fort Snelling before being
transported to the prison at Camp McClellan in Davenport,
Iowa. They were released in 1866 and sent to the Santee Reservation in Nebraska.

Charles was raised in Canada until the age of fifteen by
his grandmother and his uncle, Mysterious Medicine (Pejuta
Wakan). Jacob found Charles in Canada in 1872 and reunited
him and his grandmother with the other family members now
living within the Christian Bend in the River Dakota community near Flandreau.

Becoming Educated in Mission Schools

When Charles was brought to the Bend in the River Dakota
community, his brother John, nine years older, was well on his
way to being formally educated. In 1866 John attended the Bazile
mission school, which was organized in Santee, Nebraska, by
Rev. John P. Williamson. Williamson provided both local and
national support for the Flandreau Dakota community, serving
in the dual role of pastor and government agent. John Eastman
was at Bend in the River when the mission school in Flandreau
was being developed; then he returned to Santee and attended

what became the Santee Normal Training School, developed by Rev. Alfred L. Riggs. John became the first American Indian to attend the Beloit College Preparatory School in Wisconsin in 1871.

At Bend in the River in 1872, Charles found a community of some sixty Dakota homesteading families, building log homes and farming. The Bend in the River meetinghouse served as the initial church building and mission school until the First Presbyterian Church was built in 1873. Charles was baptized in the church, changing his name from Ohiyesa to Charles Alexander Eastman and attending the mission school for two years. In 1874 Charles enrolled at Santee Normal School back in Santee, Nebraska. His brother John was then working as a teaching assistant at this same school. In 1876 Charles also enrolled in Beloit College.

Jacob Eastman died in January 1876, four years after bringing Charles back from Canada. Jacob was buried in the First Presbyterian Church cemetery on the highest hill overlooking the valley where many of the early Dakota families settled along the banks of the Big Sioux River. For John and Charles, the year after Jacob's death was a time of reflection and recommitment to their father's wishes for their Christian education and lifestyle. John completed his required training for the ministry and was ordained in 1876 at the First Presbyterian Church. Charles would go on to complete three years of study at Beloit College.

That same year—1876, the year of Jacob's death—his brothers who had stayed in Canada took part in the Battle of the Little Bighorn, where George Armstrong Custer and his forces were wiped out. Mysterious Medicine, who raised Charles, participated, and Charles would later write an article about the battle. But John and Charles, following their father's wishes, continued learning the ways of the white man.

Rev. John Eastman, the Mentor

John became the youngest Dakota Presbyterian preacher at twenty-seven years of age. It was thought at the time that only Dakota elders had the wisdom to take on responsibility for teaching the stories and values that defined what it meant to be a good human being. John accepted the call to become a Presbyterian minister after following his father's advice to get an education, learning the language and ways of white people. The early Dakota Presbyterian ministers received training in their own language, initially from missionaries who had learned Dakota and led the effort to create the first Dakota-language dictionary. Rev. John Eastman became acceptable in the broader society as a professional: a teacher, preacher, activist, and government lobbyist for his Dakota people. He was also the mentor Charles Eastman would follow and seek advice from throughout careers that paralleled and intersected time and again.

John Eastman and Little Crow's son Wowinapi were both converted to Christianity at Camp McClellan and settled at Bend in the River. Wowinapi took the name Thomas Wakeman and worked with John Eastman to organize in 1879 the first American Indian YMCA, which was initially affiliated with the South Dakota Presbyterian Dakota Churches. In 1885 this Dakota YMCA joined the International Committee of YMCA in the United States and Canada.

Charles, in his introduction to this book, describes writing these Dakota legends from memory in 1885, while he was studying at Dartmouth, and then in 1890, when he returned from the East, conferring with John about who might confirm their accuracy. He faced a significant problem, though: in 1883 the commissioner of Indian Affairs had sent out the Code of Indian Offenses

to all Indian agents. It effectively outlawed Native religious practices, imposing stiff penalties for those who continued holding
ceremonies. Charles held on to the manuscript for many years.

John and Charles Working Together

In 1890 Charles received his medical degree at Boston College
and was assigned to the Pine Ridge Reservation as agency physician. While there, Charles witnessed the aftermath of the
Massacre at Wounded Knee Creek, where US military forces
killed nearly three hundred Lakota men, women, and children.
Eastman treated survivors, both Lakota and non-Lakota. At
Pine Ridge he met Elaine Goodale, who would become his wife,
and they started writing together.

Rev. John Eastman was at Flandreau in 1890, serving in the
capacity of a tribal liaison with the federal government, working
with political leaders, and meeting with government officials.
It was an official government position; Rev. John Williamson
had recommended him to the commissioner of Indian Affairs
in Washington. John Eastman was regularly writing letters and
meeting with local and national church and government officials. In addition, the Bend in the River YMCA he had helped
to found, along with other Native YMCAs, was successful, and
the national YMCA created a new position: national secretary
of American Indian work. John and other American Indian
members of the YMCA recommended Charles for this position,
and he accepted the job in 1894, after returning to Minnesota
and beginning to write his books.

With the publication of *Indian Boyhood* in 1903, Charles
became a national figure, and both he and John worked to edu-
cate other Americans about the Dakota people. In December
1905 John gave a speech in Washington, DC, that was published

in the *Washington Times*. He spoke about how the Flandreau Dakota community members were living in houses, farming, paying taxes, and working in politics. The Flandreau Dakota community had, indeed, come a long way from the group of Dakota families who left the Santee Reservation in Nebraska to become American Indian homesteaders. David Faribault Jr., brother-in-law of John and Charles, who was fluent in English, French, and Dakota, assumed the initial leadership role in communicating with government officials and the non-Dakota population in the area.

Charles, like John, accepted requests and responsibilities related to working on multiple Santee Sioux–related projects. John was becoming a national leader in defining the roles and responsibilities of American Indian clergy as both preachers and political activists. Charles was becoming a national leader as an American Indian physician, political activist, and author. Both brothers always defined themselves as Dakota with their knowledge of the Dakota language and stories from childhood. They also lived, as best they could, a Christian life, following their father Jacob's wishes. Both brothers are well represented by photos in suits and ties and in traditional Dakota dress holding their pipes.

Charles's books and Dakota stories became increasingly popular in the broader society. In December 1923 he was invited to join the Committee of One Hundred, an advisory council called together by the secretary of the Interior to study federal Indian policy and make recommendations for changes. This federal initiative was part of a movement away from assimilation policies, including those that banned American Indian religious customs and practices. In 1934 John Collier, the new commissioner of Indian Affairs, issued a federal policy directive allowing American Indian religious ceremonies and practices.

Charles would have been aware of these policy changes when he returned to this unpublished biblical manuscript of traditional Dakota spiritual legends and ceremonies and finished writing it in the mid-1930s, shortly before his death.

Grandma Grace and Memory Stories

My grandma Grace Eastman Moore and grandfather Oliver Shepherd Moore lived in a small two-story white house with a front porch facing the Big Sioux River. This is the house and place of my many early memories of the Bend in the River Flandreau Santee Sioux community, where my sister Linda, brother William, and I were born. Grandma Grace, as mentioned earlier, was a daughter of John Eastman and Mary Jane Faribault Eastman. Mary Jane was a daughter of Nancy McClure Faribault and David Faribault Sr.; her half brother, David Faribault Jr., married John and Charles Eastman's sister Mary. Grandpa Oliver Moore was a son of Smiley Shepherd, an admired Dakota translator and interpreter at the early Sisseton Agency, and Fannie Moore, whose father was John Mooers, a son of the well-known fur trader Hazen Mooers. Both Nancy McClure Faribault and Mary Jane Faribault Eastman in their later years lived with Grandma Grace and Grandpa Oliver in the small house facing the Big Sioux River.

The marriage union of Grandma Grace and Oliver Moore produced one child, our mother, Lillian Moore Beane. She was born in 1911 at Old Agency Village within the Sisseton Wahpeton community, now Lake Traverse Indian Reservation. Rev. John Eastman in 1906 accepted a call to become the pastor of Goodwill Presbyterian Church in Sisseton. In 1910 Grandma Grace and Grandpa Oliver moved from Flandreau to Sisseton, where Grandpa farmed for six years. The Eastman family members from Flandreau during this time reunited with Faribault and Eastman relatives already marrying and living within the Sisseton Wahpeton community. Charles would have visited this area from Washington, DC, during his years working on revising Dakota allotment roll names to ensure individual property inheritance rights. John Eastman died at his home near Old Agency Village in 1921. He was returned to Flandreau and buried in the cemetery of the First Presbyterian Church, where he had served for thirty years; his father, Jacob, is also buried there. Grandma Grace, Grandpa Oliver, my parents, and my sister are all buried in this same cemetery, along with many other relatives.

My brother and I share similar early memories of the small white house looking out toward the Big Sioux River. Grandma Grace always called Mary Jane Faribault Eastman Kunsi, the Dakota word for grandma. Kunsi was a little woman of Dakota and French blood who we came to understand spoke mostly French and Dakota. She was the first person I recall having witnessed passing away. Her wake was held in the living room of the small white house. My brother was younger and doesn't recall the wake, but he remembers passing by the bedroom adjoining the living room and seeing an old woman standing, looking out toward the Big Sioux River. He's not sure if it was Grandma McClure or Grandma Faribault, who had both lived and passed away in the house.

We both remember Grandpa Oliver gathering us kids together outside the house around a fire so we could watch him using an ax and fire to construct dugout canoes the old way. He would note when the Big Sioux River would be high enough to flood the land between the small white house and the town of Flandreau. When the flood came and the nearest road to Flandreau was underwater, his canoes were ready to

TOP: John Eastman's daughter, Grandma Grace Eastman Moore.
BOTTOM: Grandpa Oliver Moore in one of the dugout canoes he made.

ferry those willing to experience the old way of crossing the Big Sioux River. We understood from family stories that his dugout canoes were later given to families from the Sisseton Wahpeton community. The canoes would be taken back to where the river rises out of the Coteau des Prairies, starting its flow southward, connecting forever Dakota communities along its route into the Missouri River.

We were baptized in the Dakota First Presbyterian Church by Rev. Harry Jones, one of our uncles from Santee. He married Grandma Grace's sister Bessie. Many of their family members still live in Flandreau. The hymns were and still are sung in the Dakota language. Grandma Grace, having learned the piano at Santee Normal Training School, played the organ at this church. Brother William has continued that family tradition as the church organ player.

We remember being told stories about the traditional history and culture of our ancestors. Our Flandreau Santee Sioux Tribe's reservation is fifteen miles from the pipestone quarry within Pipestone National Monument in Minnesota. This place remains the most sacred place in the country, where prayer and ceremonial pipes continue to be quarried the old way. Our family often came here, returning to our Minnesota Dakota homeland and reconnecting with its spiritual center. Many of our relatives continue the tradition of making pipes from this sacred place. The Yankton Sioux Tribe has been the guardian community of the quarry by a treaty agreement with the federal government. Our father, Sidney E. Beane, was a member of the Yankton Sioux Tribe. We often went to Pipestone and walked and played throughout the quarries, listening to stories from Grandma.

Cultural Learning and Shared Family Stories

We were raised as Dakota and Christian within the Flandreau Santee Sioux Tribal Community. Grandma Grace and Grandpa Oliver were our primary cultural instructors. Their method of instruction was not the storytelling way of Smoky Day and Weyuha in the Dakota language. We were taught in English the values our grandparents found most similar between Dakota and Christian religious beliefs. These values centered on the importance of family, relationships, and prayer. We were taught to be respectful, kind, and helpful. We attended both the Dakota Indian Presbyterian church in the Dakota community and the white Presbyterian church in the town of Flandreau. Both taught us stories of a creator God and many helpers. Growing up, we never heard arguments between the two churches. The Dakota language was always present in stories and songs within our Dakota church.

Grandma Grace had signed first editions of all Charles's published books that she shared with us, along with stories of her personal relationship with Charles and Elaine Eastman. She told us about the summer she spent with Charles and Elaine at Bald Eagle Lake just north of St. Paul, Minnesota. Grandma assisted with caring for the children during the day. When Charles stopped writing, he went swimming with the children, and Grandma helped Elaine with typing his handwritten drafts. Grandma was a Dakota first speaker and writer. Grandma communicated often over the years with other members of Charles's family, including Elaine.

We attended Flandreau public school and lived on the campus of the Flandreau Indian Vocational School, run by the Bureau of Indian Affairs, during the time our parents worked there. We did not learn our Dakota history and culture in these places. Our Dakota history came from Charles Eastman's books and family stories about our ancestors coming to Bend in the River and establishing our community. Our culture emerged from stories we heard at community gatherings, often where traditional foods were shared. We experienced daily life growing up in a rural Dakota community where nature was our guide.

As we heard these stories, as we visited the pipestone quarry, we came to understand that our family had been persecuted for being Dakota and stopped openly practicing the traditional ceremonies that were outlawed after the Dakota War. Following Jacob Eastman's wishes, our family made peace with our non-Dakota neighbors, became educated in non-Dakota mission schools and public schools, and practiced Christian ceremonies and rituals. Many were similar to our Dakota ways.

Led by the examples of brothers John and Charles Eastman, our family also continued to advocate for American Indian civil rights, including the right to vote and freedom of religion. Our Dakota ancestors have always known a natural way of life based upon spiritual principles and practices, told orally as stories remembered and shared by elders. Family members have also resumed publicly practicing Dakota spiritual ceremonies previously banned. These Dakota ceremonies pray to the Creator with the vapor bath (sweat lodge) and pipe rituals. Family members have returned to the Dakota language as speakers and teachers. Our ancestors found within Christianity compatible spiritual practices that showed us a way to live in the broader society while also continuing being Dakota. John Eastman was our interpreter/guide of Christian spirituality, while Charles Eastman's writing helped sustain our Dakota spirituality.

Charles Eastman first wrote this Dakota creation cycle in Dakota, then translated it to English, as simple stories for a general audience. This book is best read for deeper understanding in concert with another of his books: *The Soul of the Indian*. Published in 1911, it provides the background material helpful for understanding many concepts, including animals as sacred beings, the "Great Mystery," ceremonial worship, and unwritten scriptures.

This unpublished manuscript has been shared among relatives to verify that the author was using the old way of teaching the stories. Dakota readers may find these stories to be deeply resonant, reflecting and connecting with other legends and spiritual practices. Dakota speakers, writers, and teachers might consider this a gift for translation back into Dakota language for even further understanding. This book also provides interested English-language readers with a chance to gain a better understanding of the Dakota spiritual worldview and the universal principles.

Continuing the Family Stories

Both my brother William and I, following Grandma Grace's wishes, have continued learning the family stories and sharing them beyond Bend in the River. William researched and wrote "An Experiment of Faith: The Journey of the Mdewakanton Dakota Who Settled on the Bend in the River." This document, completed in 2003, also includes a history of the First Presbyterian Church of Flandreau, which was recognized in 1966 as the oldest continually used church in South Dakota. He further researched and codeveloped the nationally recognized "Dakota Letters Project," which translated and exhibited letters written in Dakota by prisoners in Davenport. William has also collaborated with many other authors of books and articles that include information on the Eastman family.

Perhaps inspired by Grandma Grace's stories of Charles and John as early civil rights workers, I became involved with the Red Power Movement. I worked on civil rights issues with Native American urban communities and tribes, on both local and national levels, organizing and lobbying with the support of major church denominations and the National Council of Churches. I had the opportunity to create and coproduce the film *Native Nations: Standing Together for Civil Rights*, which aired in 2008–09 on ABC and NBC TV.

My recent film project has included major research and on-screen participation from William and my daughter Kate. *Ohiyesa: The Soul of an Indian* is a documentary film focusing on the life of Charles Eastman, produced for public television and completed in 2018. This film project brought together descendants of John Eastman and descendants of Charles and Elaine Eastman to collaborate on an Eastman family story.

In a similar fashion, Charles Alexander Eastman's new book, *In the Beginning, the Sun: The Dakota Legend of Creation*, published more than eighty years after his death, includes essays written by descendants of the three brothers, Charles, John, and David. This collection further expands the circle of Eastman family members speaking together about who we are and the stories we share.

PART 2
THE DAKOTA LEGEND
OF CREATION

SIOUX MYTHOLOGY

THE INDIANS' BIBLE

THE STORY OF THE CREATION

By

Charles Alexander Eastman
(Ohiyesa)

- -

The title page of Charles Alexander Eastman's typescript.

Introduction

CHARLES ALEXANDER EASTMAN (OHIYESA)

IN PRESENTING THE SIOUX MYTHOLOGY OR THE CREATION Legend, the author makes no pretense of literary effort. The main purpose is to offer the Legend in its simplicity and entirety, the successive stories of the eras and epochs, in the progression of the Creation, the material, the animal, and finally the man.

Second, all care is taken to maintain the manner of teaching, by the native legend repeaters, who were especially selected by the council of each tribe or band, for the work.

Third, the author, himself, is a thorough pupil and student of one of the best teachers of the Sioux nation, namely Smoky Day, before he entered civilization. He was especially fortunate in this respect, and in not having passed through the disastrous period of the transitional reservation life, which was the undoing of the customs and cultural training of the race, which were founded and developed for untold centuries on their faith in their peculiar philosophy of life, derived from these legends.

These legends were first written from memory, while the author was yet a student at Dartmouth College in 1885, in the Sioux language.

When he returned from the East in 1890, with the help of his brother, Rev. John Eastman, he learned that there were then only three old men living, who were able to repeat the Creation Legend, the Sacred Ritual, consecutively, namely: Weyuha of the Wahpeton Sioux; Chantanhotonka of the Mde-Wakontonwan Sioux (who fled to Canada during the outbreak of 1862, in Minnesota, and was then living near Prince Albert, Saskatchewan); and Tawicinduta, a Wahpekuta Sioux (inter-married among the Yanktonais Sioux). All of them were very old then, save Weyuha.

With the help of his brother John and Weyuha's son, Robert Hopkins, the author was able to induce the old sage to review his manuscript. He was much pleased that it was correct, save in the detail stories. He then consented to deliver the twelve lessons. When he met the listeners for the first lesson, he said to them, "You will have to represent my last pupils; I will teach you as I used to the children of the tribe, and you must think yourself living in that former day." The author requested him to follow the lessons of his last class that he had, before he was deprived of his pupils. He did.

In this manner, the author secured his system of teaching, which is given entire in this volume.

Thirty-five years ago, there were a few old men and women who could repeat one or another of the epochs of the animal kingdom, but not comprehensively, and there were some who could repeat some of the animal stories and of Unktomi and that regime. But they were isolated, not only in the manner the forces of civilization came upon them, but also by the efforts of the government and the missionaries, who in order to civilize quickly, have succeeded in silencing their teachers and all Indianism. This assertion is not for criticism, but a reason for the loss of Indian philosophy.

In recent years there has been much effort made to secure what the Indian had developed, but the seers are dead and gone, and the young Indian who is forced from home to government school has no knowledge of his people's teachings and philosophy.

It is the earnest desire of the author to present in this book the basis of his people's philosophy and religion, out of which they had derived all their customs and the motive for their actions.

The reason these legends were not given to the public before, is that the public had not progressed to the present-day attitude. Now, I feel they are ready to accept them in broader consideration and appreciation of the principles which the natives developed.

Author

[Charles Alexander Eastman (Ohiyesa), about 1935]

1

The Sun, the Earth, the Moon, and the Earth's First Children

WEYUHA WAS MUCH LOVED AND HONORED BY HIS PEOPLE. He had already lived through seventy-two winters, although he was very active and much younger in appearance. He possessed a gentle and winning disposition. With these gifts, he had been recognized by the Sioux tribe of which he was a member as an able and respected man, and the best informed and trained in the lore of his people.

The old sage, Shungilasapa (Black Fox) had just resigned his office or position, as the keeper and teacher of the tribal lore. Sometimes in such events, it was not easy to find a man suited for the duties involved in the office, to assume the sacred position; therefore, it was fortunate for the tribe to have among them Weyuha, the genial storyteller. Thus, he was appointed to succeed the aged Shungilasapa when he was seventy-two. At the time this story was repeated, Weyuha had just passed his ninetieth year.

"Those who once heard him would never forget him and his story, and would always want to hear him again," said one of the men in the council. Throughout the teepee village the appointment was announced by the tribe's criers.

As the summer drew to a close, the parents of the best and well-ordered families had their children started for the first lesson of the Creation story to be given by the new teacher, Weyuha. (These stories were never told in the summer.)

The motley groups of children, painted with all colors of the rainbow, wrapped in blankets and dressed in doeskin shirts or gowns, approached the teacher's buffalo-skin teepee. They found him sitting under an aged spreading oak tree which stood near his teepee, ready for them.

"Ah ha! You are very good children to come so promptly. This shows that your parents are good—they love their children. They wish for you to know the true story of life.

"I presume you have been told by your parents that we have a few rules to keep us in order while we are engaged in the study of the Legend of Life. One is that no one must talk or whisper. Another is that one must not ask questions while I repeat the tales. Such things would disturb and confuse your memories. And the more important one is that you agree to have your parents or grandparents have you repeat word for word each day's lessons on your return home. Only in this way, can you expect to retain the Creation story and profit by the philosophy it teaches. For in the lives of the animals and man, the Creator provided for everything and the laws of physical life were ordered like a double-bladed knife. It cuts both ways. All things are made for us; therefore they are for usefulness and good, but the misuse of them cuts. It reacts against us. Enough is sufficient. Excess of anything causes the trouble of the mind. These laws controlling our physical well-being were bound in a narrow trail. It requires of us to keep in the middle of the path. In other words, we must practice moderation in all our habits.

"The Great Mystery is the ruler of our world. His spirit we called the Great Spirit. But all these truths will become clearer to your mind, as we go along with the Legend of the Creation. This Legend comes to us from our ancestors. It must have started somewhere in far-off times. From it, we conceived and formed all our customs, social and spiritual.

"First place, we love and believe in the Great Mystery, because He is our God, Creator and Father. We think He dwells, thinks, and moves in all His creations. He is everywhere at once, and in all times. We are all alike in His sight, save in reference to our daily conduct, our thinking, and our behavior.

"In order that our people may always be fully supplied with the truths and principles of life, we teach our young people the story of the Creation before they become headstrong, before they reach young manhood and young womanhood and become drunk with their youthful strength. It is necessary for them to have light and wisdom. Then they cannot blame anyone but themselves when misfortune overtakes them. Readiness to make excuses we consider a weakness in a person. Such a one is at the door of falsehood.

"Now my children, these are the things that developed in the story and life of the animals and men."

The Legend of Creation

In the beginning, the Sun, a handsome, noble, and brave young man, was one of the children of the Great Mystery. He was given the liberty to travel and to find a country of his own to rule. He went away courageously and confidently, because he was young and strong. But his father had warned him not to lose himself by yielding to the love of a woman, nor to associate with one too intimately, until he understood himself and her, too.

When he had traveled all over the great country of the sky and had seen everything there was to be seen, he became lonely, because he was true to his father's warning. Because he was so handsome, brilliant, and magnetic, many star maidens made love to him. He resisted them all, but they pursued him wherever he went. He had seen many wonderful people, but he kept himself far away from them.

At last he came to a new and vast country. He liked it much and lingered there. Behold! All at once there appeared before him two beautiful maidens—the Earth and the Moon. They were two sisters.

They seemed to him very refined and modest, and different from those he had seen. Also, they did many kind things for him. He was quite charmed and fascinated. He was scarcely able to retain his self-possession. "But surely," he thought, "I have been true to my father's warning; he would now excuse me if I do fall in love." So he asked the older of the two maidens, the Earth, to be his wife.

In time they were wedded and were very happy, for the two will rule the country in which they found each other and are to start a race of people. The young man, the Sun, had told his beautiful wife that the rules of his life, as set by his father, prohibited them from living too close together, and she, therefore, must be content to remain at a certain distance in his presence.

The Earth was very anxious to make her husband happy, so she obeyed, and there seemed to be no hardship on either of them until one summer day she wanted him to tell her all about his people and his plans for the future. The Sun also loved his young wife, and to please her he consented. As he was talking, his wife, being so much in love, unthinkingly came too close to her husband. In a moment she was caught in a flame of fire. She screamed for help, but all he could do was to flee from her, which he did.

Her sister, the Moon, who also heard her distress, came running to her rescue. She threw vessels of water upon her body until the flame was put out. However, the Earth was terribly burned. The Moon, very naturally, was kind to her sister. She nursed and attended all her needs for many years, for the Earth was an invalid for a long time. The young sister was accustomed to wash all the wounds and sores of her sister's body. For a long time the Earth's body was kept under water to relieve the pains, except her head, and gradually other parts of her emerged from the water.

One day the Moon discovered that the blood and particles that were washed off from her sister's wounds and fell into the water became tiny little creatures. There were many, many of them. She was at first startled, but after a while, she told her sister.

"Ah," replied the sick Earth, "I am glad; they are my babes." She assured her sister, "My handsome husband loves me so much, and I adore him; this is the result."

"But, my dear sister," the Moon replied, "there are so many of them, the water is just full of them, swimming in groups."

"Yes, Sister, then they will not be lonesome," Earth answered.

"How can you feed them all?" the other asked.

"Ah, my sister, the Great Mystery has given me plenty of milk for them," Earth cheerfully answered. "They will never go hungry, unless they are careless children," she added.

"But, my sister, the little creatures will make you poor; you will not be so beautiful as you were before this happened," said the Moon. "They will soon make you old and wrinkled," further remarked the Moon maiden.

"Ah, but my husband, the Sun, and I will get along with them somehow; besides, his father, the Great Mystery, is not only wise but very rich. He will guide us," she assured.

After a thoughtful silence, the Moon said, "There is no use

worrying now, I suppose. They are born to you, and I imagine we must take good care of them. I will help you all I can while you are sick, and I must love them."

While the Earth was sick, the Sun was keeping on constant watch from a distance, and the Moon was between the two so that there would be no more mishaps to disturb their peace. Her shadows always soothed her sister's body. After a long time, the Earth recovered her health, but she was not so beautiful as before her misfortune. Indeed, she had many scars and wrinkles.

By this time, her water children were many. In fact, some of them had grown quite large, but there were still others later born who were little. Many of the more active ones often came out of the water and sat and played on her body. They soon noticed how their mother had been badly burned, and some of her bones were exposed. One day they asked their aunt, the Moon, saying, "Do you not think we might bring up some of mother's flesh from down in the bottom of the water, where she does not need it, to cover her exposed bones on the surface?"

Moon replied, "Yes, you must love your mother—that will comfort and make her happy."

So in this way, all her children, millions of them, went to work for their mother to cover her exposed bones with materials brought from under the water. In this connection, there are many legends in which animals claim being the first who thus brought earth, but the Legend says that every animal, little or big, helped in this work. By this loving work of her children, the Earth regained some of her original beauty, and of course she was very glad to realize that her children loved her.

During the sickness of the Earth, among the many duties of the Moon was putting the children to sleep with lullabies, which the mosquitoes still sing. All the while Moon was nursing her sister, she wore a white veil, so that she would not cause any irritation in her sister's body by her bright light. This is why we see the moon to this day in a pale light, through her veil.

When all the children of the Earth brought substance from the bottom of the water to cover the exposed parts of her body, they made the Land and the longest and biggest pools of water we know as the Ocean, and the little ones are called the Lakes. These are many, scattered all over her body. From these, waters ran away to the Ocean to live, and these we called the Rivers. Their many trails are in turn used by the sky waters. The latter is supposed to be the work of the Moon, so that the Sun will not set fire on her sister again, and also to make a home for some of the water animals.

*

Here then is the beginning of family life, with all its attending happiness, drawbacks, and sorrows. It means activity—work to keep the family going.

My good children, I know your minds are full of questions, but you have been very good and patient. Those "whys" which are disturbing you will explain themselves as we go on with the Legend. (Good old Weyuha had noticed by their expressions what they had suffered.) You must remember, my children, he resumed, this legend of the Sun, Earth, and Moon and their children is like a tree. We must learn first about the root, the trunk, and its branches. Then, later, we shall take up its leaves, the flowers, and the seed.

The Great Mystery came and reproached the Sun, His son. He commanded him never to come too close to the Earth again. So it has been ever since.

When the Great Mystery viewed the situation brought about by the marriage of the Sun with the Earth, He knew there would be a world of people. Then and there, He laid down the rules and laws for their bodies and minds. He limited the length of life of the body in each tribe, for if He did not do that, the Earth would soon find she had no room for them all. He made laws according to the conditions in which each tribe lived.

He ordained that all the children will receive from their parents substance and energy, and He will give them the Spirit. That means the Earth gives them body; the Sun gives them heat or energy, while He gives them the breath. He provided in the body of each tribe organs peculiar to them, adequate to function in obedience to His laws. The mind is to be evolved in the body by the influence of the Spirit. The true Spirit or soul spirit is the true mind, and is always clear, but the body mind is not always true or clear, because it is influenced by matter or material things based on human experience.

He put the Spirit in the seed of the male, and the woman develops it. This spirit seemed to be the imperishable part of the body, and departs when the body is killed or dies. Spirit is to the mind like the Sun is to its ray of light. He distributed the gifts to all His creatures according to their nature and habits and modes of life or condition in and by which they live. He made it possible for individuals in every tribe to develop their body, mind, and spirit in progress.

His laws of sustenance were very strict. While everything was given for the maintenance of the body, the physical well-being, the abuse of them becomes dangerous to the body. The mind is governed by laws peculiar to itself for its progress and happiness. But the soul mind is the light that guides true.

My children, this is a long tale—I know you are tired. I will stop here, and may the good spirit—the soul spirit—guide you in your study of the Creation story. I will give you two days in which to repeat and rehearse our first lesson.

2

Unktomi and the Killing of Eayah, the Devourer

WE ARE HAPPY TODAY, BECAUSE THE SUN IS BRIGHT AND warm, because we are healthy and well cared for. Our thanks are first to the Great Mystery; second, to the Sun and the Earth, our physical grandparents; and third, to our loving memories and to those who have departed, especially our relatives. These are our daily thanks. Sometimes, in our hunting, we appeal to the spirits; this is also true in warfare, but that is special, and they are the lesser spirits, because the motive is selfish. In the progress of this Legend, we will find out why these customs are observed by our people.

We will now come to the legend of the Earth's first children and what occurred during the period they controlled the Earth. As I have told you, these animal people who were the first children of the Earth had multiplied themselves in such numbers that both the water and the land were well inhabited by them. But this took ages of time. The Earth, too, in the meantime, had fully recovered and was as beautiful as we see it now. Yet it was no small matter for the Earth and the Sun to provide food for them all, and to rule them peacefully. Many of them were prolific in producing children of their own. In this way many tribes of animals came into existence. There were as many tribes as there were different kinds of grass and trees. All believed themselves the best and favorite children of their parents, the Sun and the Earth. These tribes had grown up in a variety of sizes and with differing powers of intellect, each claiming superiority in form of body and attractiveness, as well as in intelligence.

Here then was the beginning of the difficulties between brothers and brothers, so too between sisters and sisters—difficulties that were inherited by their children. Every succeeding generation increased and widened this bad spirit, and antagonism between tribes, families, and individuals. It seems it became a trait in all animals and in man.

At first, the motives for these differences were fundamental things such as food, love, and self-protection. Right and wrong were white and black. Up to this time, Mother Earth had fed them all with her own substance; they did nothing to maintain themselves, and even fought over the supply she had provided them. It was very trying and perplexing for the parents.

The Sun and the Earth finally appealed to the Great Mystery for help. Then it was that the laws governing their children's lives were readjusted. First, the Great Mystery arranged them in two divisions: the water people and the land people. He then limited the sphere of their lives, so that one group could not interfere with another group too easily. Even then, there were still difficulties arising among each set. Therefore there was still the necessity of further limiting the strong from taking advantage of the weaker and smaller tribes. The best method of meeting these countless difficulties was a puzzle, even for the Great Mystery, for a while.

At last, He decided to give each tribe weapons of defense and protection, which also might be used as a means for providing themselves with food and shelter. He gave some sharp teeth, others horns or claws; still others, swift running or swimming or strength. He again limited them in the use of these weapons under certain conditions, so that none could be entirely at the mercy of another. This applies to tribes as well as individuals.

For instance, a tribe physically small and helpless against the strength of a powerful enemy, being small, can get away quickly or hide easily to escape danger. Even their colors may be used in this manner.

In this way, each had its advantages and disadvantages, which in effect equalized and balanced their powers. Likewise, this was true of their mental capacity. Some had the ability to think or reason, while others were endowed with finer instincts and intuition.

Thus once more the Sun and the Earth started with their many and unruly children. For ages they seem to have progressed fairly well. But the tribes became too many. In spite of all the kind provisions and efforts of the Earth mother, many of her tribes were on the verge of starvation. Then she discovered, to her distress, that the larger and stronger tribes, in their predicament, began to eat the smaller and weaker tribes; some even did this among their tribes. This latter was cannibalism, and shocked Mother Earth. She told her husband, the Sun, what was happening. He reproached and punished some severely, but that did not stop them. The parents dared not tell nor ask help of the Great Mystery. And so it was continued, from that far-off time to this day.

When the Great Mystery had provided each tribe with weapons for protection and self support, He had supplied them also with permanent coloring of their garments, for they were all naked children, like the baby mouse, up to that time. To some, He gave warm clothing in furs and feathers; to others He gave waterproof coats with scales; others nicely thick coats. He painted and embroidered these garments beautifully. In some of the coats He used only one color; in others He employed two, while in others He used many brilliant colors. He had some of them change their colors every season, but most of them once a year. This is why the animals shed their hair, and the birds lose their feathers for new ones, while the snakes just crawl out of their surface skin for a fresher one.

Sometimes the question arises among us as to why the Great Mystery made so many ridiculous and peculiar creatures, and why he painted some of them so grotesquely and others so superfluously. The answer, we think, is that He is an artist and full of humor at times. He made these for His own amusement with the waste material. It is hard to find why some creatures are made, but after all, that concerns the Great Mystery alone.

The Earth, after having gone through many thrilling experiences with their children, felt quite happy and concluded to bear the troubles with them, and do the very best she could for them, when there grew up two children of unusual intelligence and character. These were Unktomi and Eayah. They became rivals. They were self-appointed chiefs of all the animal people. Each declared that he was the oldest child born on Earth, therefore the wisest whom all must consult in tribal affairs.

All the legends of the various nations relating to this animal world lead us to believe that Unktomi was the son of the Crab and a Water Spider princess. So he was called the "Spider."

He was gifted in eloquence and a great logician, and withal possessed a certain amount of prophetic power, as well as much dramatic talent. He was genial and very friendly with everyone. But he was also a political schemer and very ambitious. He not only used all his talent and knowledge, but would stoop to low and unprincipled means to advance his personal fortunes. He was resourceful and possessed much tact in all his schemes. Scarcely ever was he openly resentful or impatient, for with all his contradictory traits, he was extremely polite and genial, indeed often generous and sympathetic. Thus his actions were often puzzling and strangely human.

The name "Unktomi" was given him because he possessed a genius for weaving falsehood as daintily as his namesake, the spider, weaves exquisite patterns in cobwebs to snare unwary victims.

Even in our own day if anyone shows a gift for falsifying we called him Unktomi. In nearly all our stories of the Creation, Unktomi is involved. On this account some of the Indian tribes who are not well versed in the true Legend confused Unktomi with the Great Teacher, Eshnaicage, whose protection and counsel guided the first man from birth. We shall hear of him later.

Eayah, the contemporary and rival of Unktomi, was altogether a different character. He was supposed to be a cross between Chief Pike and Princess Green Frog. He was loathsome and cruel. Physically and mentally, he was quite the opposite of his genial rival, being tall but with an immense stomach. His head was ill-shaped, with small piercing green eyes and a mouth so big that it extended from ear to ear. Surly, sullen, and evil-tempered, he was never known to show a pleasant smile. When he did laugh, it sounded strangely mirthless. His ambition was to rule the whole animal kingdom so that he might have a whole tribe for lunch to appease his horrible hunger.

Like Unktomi, he had a certain amount of magic power. No one seemed to have the power to destroy him. This magic life made Eayah a powerful and dangerous creature to the animal people.

But Unktomi, eventually, cunningly outwitted and killed him. Eayah had been in the habit of feasting on innocent people. Sometimes he swallowed a whole herd of buffalo, or a lake full of waterfowl or fish, if they did not watch him closely. Thus he terrorized all the animals.

Unktomi, with his ambition to be a hero, had been watching

for an opportunity to overpower his rival so that he might then be the wisest man among the animal people. He had to be shrewd and clever to accomplish his purpose.

One day Eayah visited Unktomi unexpectedly, but it was impossible to surprise him, for he was alert and a good scout, although pretending otherwise. After he had cordially received Eayah and smoked with him, Unktomi advised his guest to take a nap while he was preparing a great feast for him.

During their conversation, Unktomi had cleverly learned that thunder and lightning frightened Eayah, and that he could only be destroyed through his stomach, because of his greed. So the wily host went out and called a council of all the animals, but they were afraid to come near Eayah. He asked them to be brave and to do what he desired them to do without delay, and no harm would befall them.

He had the Bears, Wolves, Hawks, and Otters gather all the oyster shells and eels they could find and bring them to his teepee. The Raccoons, Minks, and Skunks, whom Unktomi had overlooked in his haste, also volunteered their service. At the same time, he sent the Cliff Swallow as a messenger to the Thunder Spirit, to have him start on the war path above them at a given signal from below.

Having completed all the preparations, Unktomi woke Eayah for the feast. He got up, rubbing his eyes, and then stretched himself and gave a yawn, which scared the animals, but the host cleverly quieted them.

Behold, the feast! Hills of oysters and eels concealed in piles of seaweed, mixed with quick-lime and saturated in water-oil (kerosene) from the swamps.

"Now," said Unktomi, "my good friend, I have some fine appetizers for you. When you finish them I have a herd of buffalo for your meat. Open your mouth and close your eyes." When

Eayah opened his mouth, the animals lost no time in throwing armfuls of food into the cavity of the glutton's stomach, until all was used up.

Very soon after, Eayah asked for water. Again, the animals diligently brought him much water. Behold, the honored guest was laboring under difficulties. His loud groans shook the hills. He held onto his stomach and shouted, "Unktomi, you have poisoned me!" to which Unktomi replied, "Within hearing of all these people I say to you, I gave you only what they themselves considered good food. I am not guilty." By this time Eayah was dying in agony, when suddenly the heaven was clouded and thunder and lightning started. A loud clash came, and Eayah was dead.

"Yet even today, my children," said Weyuha, the teacher, "it is believed by our people that the spirit of Eayah still roams in this world, and sometimes enters into the body of some of the animals, and even in human beings. Therefore, when a child is born, its throat and tongue are carefully examined. For Eayah, too, has a place in many of the legends, because some of his characteristics appear in the traits of men, and therefore he is studied with care and caution."

Thus ended the second lesson.

3

Unktomi's Travels and the First Mourning

THE DEATH OF EAYAH WAS RECEIVED WITH JOY AND RELIEF throughout the world, especially among the more active animals who furnished a bigger meal. When he was struck by the lightning, none went near his body for fear he might rise up and, in his madness, destroy them. In time, when they were convinced that he was really killed, they approached to give him a decent burial. "But," Unktomi said, "since he is beaten, he is in your power. You must make a great fire, for we shall cremate his body and scatter the ashes to the four winds, so he can never come back to life again." In this manner Eayah's body was disposed of. "In this way," said Unktomi, "the Thunder War Chief will keep his spirit in prison forever."

The whole world was now cleared for Unktomi's control, for had he not cleverly disposed of the greatest physical enemy to the animal kingdom? They must show their gratitude and appreciation of his daring and bravery, in spite of their distrust of his schemes.

In a great council of the land animals, he was honored and thanked for the work he had accomplished. They declared that all the tribes would always be friendly and tolerate him, but they reserved the right to rule and manage their own affairs. This was done to check him from assuming too much authority over them, because they knew him to be a politician and fortune hunter as well as a gambler, and should he have control over them, he would bring trouble and grief.

Unktomi, on the other hand, was well aware of the working of their minds; he told them they need not worry about him. He would be perfectly satisfied, he said, if they would allow him to select one of their princesses for his wife. He declared himself contented to retire to a quiet family life.

The chiefs of all the animals met in council to consider his proposition. After a debate, they decided to offer him Princess Toad. "For," they said, "it is not wise to give him the privilege of selecting one out of all of them." But the secret reason was that if he allied himself to the Toad people, Unktomi's activities would be limited and his children would not be feared, because the Toads were a conservative and quiet people. Thus, in time, he would be old and less liable to trouble them. In any event, this marriage will settle him for the present. He was, to their pleasant surprise, satisfied. It was well known that one of his ambitions was to secure the most beautiful woman of all the animal people for his wife.

For a long time, Unktomi lived with the Toads, where he was found to be a very poor hunter. As a result, his family was very poor, his children always hungry. But he apologized to his father-in-law by explaining that his father was a great Medicine man who taught him to be, like himself, a great Medicine man and never trained him in the skill of hunting. "Besides, he and I do not believe in killing."

His wife finally took her children and left him, saying, "You are not a man like other men, to raise respectable children."

He replied, "It is ordered that a wise man should not devote his time to raising children; his work is for all the people."

This condemnation of his Toad wife had branded him as a worthless family man, which became known to all the people of the world. On this account, no self-respecting woman would marry him. He had to disguise himself, to secure a decent woman. With all his shrewdness and ability of mind, with his world experience and magic power, he was denied the privilege of making himself handsome and attractive.

Unktomi's life among the Toad people was full of events and activity. He knew that the Toads, Turtles, and Reptiles were allied nations, and they constituted one of the wisest and strongest of all the confederations of tribes of the Earth's children. From this branch of the race both Unktomi and Eayah had come. Now Eayah was gone; there was no one to contest his leadership.

He had lost no time in presenting himself before the council of wise men of the tribe. This was not the custom of the tribe, for a newcomer, almost a stranger, to force himself upon the council. It was a serious breach of their conservative customs and laws. This displeased them very much, and they declared among themselves that the land animals had played unfair to the Toad-Turtle-Reptile tribes.

Of course Unktomi had known how they would feel about his assumption of leadership, so he was ready to explain. "It is true, age is to be respected, and wisdom must be the guide in all tribal affairs," he declared. "And," said he with much dignity, "he who has these qualities has the natural right to participate in any council of any people. Besides, by the right of birth, I should rule, for I am a descendant of your great Medicine man, Crab, and the beautiful Princess Spider. But I was born before that; I was the first child of the Earth and the Sun. Therefore I have these gifts, more than any other, from them. Have I not outwitted Eayah, your greatest enemy?" No one dared to refute his statement; all were quietly and silently smoking. "I challenge any among you to say, what I say is not true."

At last the Sea Turtle Medicine man of great age got up; "Unktomi, it is not given in our Sacred Ritual that you were the first born, and that you were appointed to have the privilege to appear in any council of any tribe, although a stranger. The tribes of the world have their customs and laws given to them by the Great Mystery to guide them in their affairs; they know no other rules or laws."

"That is true," Unktomi answered him, "but that does not prove what I say is not true. How did you come to be councilor? Is it not because you have attained a great age and store up much knowledge and have been useful during your lives? Have I not been useful to all and taught youth the truth of life? You are bound by the customs of your tribe alone. I am free to all," replied Unktomi triumphantly.

The whole council was again in deep silence, and their silence admitted that he spoke the truth.

So he became a member of the great council, the disturbing member in all their tribal councils; but in the end, his eloquence and logic always convinced them against their better judgment.

Meanwhile, he was availing himself of the opportunity to learn all their laws and medicines for use, should the occasion arise. And eventually, the people became more accustomed to his peculiarities and eccentricities.

While he was occupied deeply in the affairs of the tribes, and stored up much knowledge and had many experiences, there were times when he pretended to be very sad and grieved over the loss of his wife and children, although he was an optimist and never lost sleep or worried over ill luck or misfortune. He always said to himself, "There is another day coming."

The whole nation was camping together at the Great Water (ocean), where there was much pine and deep forest by high bluffs. It was a celebration and welcome to Miniyatapi (the whale) and his warriors to appear on the Great Water.

There was a great council, and of course Unktomi in high

spirits wanted to display his eloquence and cleverness, when a messenger, a pigeon, appeared bringing news of a battle between the Rattle Snakes, an outlawed tribe, and the Toads, in which a whole band of Toads were massacred. When the names of the families killed were made known, Unktomi's wife and sons were included. The news shocked him. He sat silent in the council. Finally, he slowly got up from the council and camp and walked away into the deep woods.

Meanwhile, Miniyatapi and his water warriors came. They displayed their powers by shooting sprays of water skyward like arrows, and they jumped great heights from the big waves. All the tribes on shore gave the war whoop to cheer them. This exhibition over, the water warriors lay upon the surface of the water to watch the dances and sports of the land people. Millions of the land and water people were there.

Behold. Unktomi appeared before them all, walking alone along the shore. He was singing a dirge and wailing alternately. He disrobed, removed all his feathers and ornaments, slashed his legs and arms so that he was bleeding profusely, while his hair was cut short and his face painted black. Unktomi thus mourned and grieved. All the water warriors disappeared in an instant, and the land animals stopped their celebration.

The men wailed or sang dirges and the women wailed with them.

This was the first mourning ever known. It was Unktomi's mourning. The custom was thus established which our people have followed ever since.

4

Unktomi's Journey to the Bottom of the Sea and the Sacred Ritual

WHEN THE CHILDREN ARRIVED, THEY FOUND WEYUHA WITH two guests, Matohuta and Chantewakan (Grizzly Bear and Sacred Heart). These two were repeaters of legends of their respective tribes. "How, how, my good children! We have with us today two great Medicine men of our nation. They have taught, many years, these very stories to the youths of their tribes. I am glad to have this honor of their presence. They have the right to correct me if I make any mistakes." This introduction of the two old men made the children be serious and show deep respect and reverence by their conduct.

We have finished in the last lesson the unfortunate destruction of Unktomi's family, and the beginning of our people's custom of mourning. We shall now follow him in his departure and wanderings in another world. He had, however, spent a long time with the people who, part of the time, live in water and land—the Toad-Turtle-Reptile nations. But the time had come for him to visit other parts of the world. He felt he must present himself to other nations, who live in entirely different customs and conditions. While he had, as I told you, in the start of his career, certain magic gifts, he does not use them commonly. He follows the usages and customs as he found them among the different nations of the Earth. He usually, on the start, gets himself adopted into the tribe and in time, by skillful tactics, secures a wife; then he claims relations with the tribe. Herein he exposes himself to the whims and biases of the members of the tribe concerned; also he urges them to make him over like themselves. Consequently, they would make him the most humble-looking and ungraceful person possible. In this way, he conformed to their ways in every respect. This was of course a drawback and disadvantage to him, in any effort of leadership on his part.

"They were much afraid, if they made me any way near decent looking, all their pretty maidens would fall in love with me. But I will fool them in that, too, whenever I choose," he boastfully remarked. It is believed that his looks and makeup often help him in playing the rogue and the funny man. Indeed, he was clownish and ridiculously foolish when it is his gain to play the role, in order to carry out some of his schemes. His resourcefulness, with much dry wit and humor, were the secret power in swaying the minds of the people he was dealing with for the moment.

When Unktomi made up his mind to visit and explore the underwater world, he looked about and along the shore for a start. He found that the big Water Turtle had just been appointed to visit the Great Medicine People of the Ocean. He first found a lazy dogfish, basking in the sun-warmed shallow water. "Ah, ah, my good and handsome friend," he addressed him, "you are the happiest, ease-loving man of the world. See how peacefully you are enjoying the warm sun, while the gentle waves soothe your senses. I would give anything if you will adopt me," quoth he.

"You are mistaken, I have the hardest life of all the people of the water world. Not only no one wants my company, but they would chase me from shore to shore. I had to flee to the shallow water to save my life," he replied.

"Ah my good friend, think how you lie here without any

exertion. Your food is brought to you. All the juicy little fish and the omelets of fish eggs lying around you. What other hunter can find his meal so easy? Besides, I can be of some service to you," urged Unktomi.

"You do not realize the hardship I have; even when I am here at the shore, I never can sleep with both eyes closed, because the Hawks and some of the land animals will cruelly drag me out of the water."

But Unktomi was so persistent that Witko (Drunk), the dogfish, had to adopt him. Under a beautiful pine-clad cliff, one sunny day, Witko and Unktomi were basking on the warm pebbly shore; Witko had had a strenuous night in fighting a garfish. He was bruised and full of wounds; therefore he had hardly closed one eye when Unktomi flashed his tail with a whoop, a warning for danger; at the same instant he darted for the deep water, in a streak, for safety. Witko followed without any chance to see what was the danger. When, breathlessly, they reached the bottom, he inquired what was the trouble. Unktomi declared they had had the narrowest escape of their lives. "I saw the shadow of a big hawk diving for us from the sky," he said. "Ugh," said the dogfish, "I only saw a dragonfly going by. You must be a mosquito to fear a dragonfly."

This had happened so often that poor Witko had no rest at all. Finally he disowned and discharged him. In this manner, Unktomi had himself made into all the water tribes. But he had a definite object in his scheme—that was to reach the bottom of the Great Water. Meanwhile, he stayed long enough with each tribe so that he learned their customs.

While he was going on this journey, he took pains to note all the different tribes and the country in which they lived. He sometimes called these people "the canoe people," for, he said, "their bodies are living canoes and they have not only waterproof garments, but most beautifully painted and embroidered clothing. None of them have real legs and feet or wings, but they do have all kinds of paddles, which are attached on various parts of their bodies, so that they can go to any part of their water country." Yet there were some who lived deep in the bottom of the Big Water who have legs; some of them have many legs, horns, and claws, big and strong enough to pull up a big oak tree by the roots.

Also, among the many different tribes Unktomi found some of the Toad-Turtle-Reptile race, who were chiefs down there. These were very big—some of them being as big as three buffalo. To his happy surprise, Unktomi had found his great-great . . . grandparents on both sides; his mother and father were down there; they were very, very large. But they did not recognize him as their descendant. He was afraid to speak to them, because they were powerful.

In his trip, all the way down, he passed many broad prairies, plains, hills, mountains, and high cliffs, and some with heavy forests. He observed, too, many kinds of beautiful flowers.

The great chiefs of the Medicine people lived in cave teepees built with many beautiful stones and shells of every color. Many of the little people who lived on the shelves of the big teepee of the chiefs are painted so they looked like the stones with which the chiefs' teepees were built.

The Sea Turtle Medicine man in whose company Unktomi went on this historic trip looked like an insignificant and common little man, compared with these great chiefs. It was a very hard journey, but every tribe they visited provided them with the ways and means to reach and enter the next country, and guides and passwords were given them.

For once he was puzzled and bewildered. He was uncertain about what sort of diplomacy he should adopt, for these conservative and wise old nations were autocrats of the animal people. It would not do for him to try his bluffing tactics on their wisdom and ripe old age. Also, they have lived for ages nearer to the heart of the good Mother Earth; therefore they possessed greater gifts in knowledge and understanding of physical life. And the spirit that the Great Mystery invested in the Earth and the Sun was stored in them, he thought.

On the way, all along their trip, they seemed to have traveled downward. Every time they entered a country, Unktomi thought that was the last one, but soon they would reach the edge of a great mountain range, or a lofty palisade of cliffs, beyond a vast prairie. As they progressed on the trail, the views became darker, because the light became lesser.

When they approached the last precipice, they could hardly see the country beyond. There they met the scouts of the chief people. Miniwancakeya (the Sea Turtle) held the medicine-pipe to them with prayer, and gave the pass signs (pass-words). They said, to their surprise, all the chief Medicine men knew the moment they started on this journey. Miniwancakeya and Unktomi were put into the sacred sweat lodge and made to repeat the sacred vows. Thus they were prepared for the admission to the country or abode of the autocrats of the children of the Earth, whom she kept close to her heart.

All this time, Unktomi was thinking hard. He was given power, and skill in reasoning and logic and philosophy, which concern the animal people on the surface of the Earth. But he found a new race under different surroundings, and powerful, because they lived much longer lives and so close to the heart and soul of the Earth. They have solved all problems which concern the peoples of the Earth. On the other hand, he felt that the nations on the surface of Mother Earth are air bubbles, quickly born, as quickly lived out and returned again to their mother.

They are sunshine children; therefore they are transparent in body and mind, besides being frail and delicate, he thought. For these reasons also, they are active, quick in reasoning, but superficial and changeable. These people reasoned deeply and solved all the roots and trunks of the big problems. These thoughts were quickly passed through Unktomi's mind. In fact, all the treasures of the Earth, too, were lying about them. The most beautiful, brilliant, durable colors were there; even the flowers scarcely fade there, while the clothing of the people does not change every year and season.

Thus the quick mind of the wily Unktomi noticed and compared these things. It was a strong reasoning that convinced him to assume an attitude of ignorance and patronization for his role. Therefore he presented himself as a faithful man reverently seeking the truth and knowledge, and that he was nothing but an attendant and fellow-traveler of the Medicine man, Miniwancakeya. In this way, he shrewdly and diplomatically played second part.

His political scheming mind recognized the wonderful opportunity to secure deep knowledge and understanding from the wise and staid Medicine Men and their treasure house. Their ritual and sacred customs will be an immense store of resources for him to rely on and draw from in his trickery, which was his part in the teaching as well as establishing customs and societies among the surface people. To be sure, he had learned and secured much information in this trip, and he was already familiar with all the laws and customs of the upper world; yet he was not an authority on them. That is, he was not allowed. "The Sun must have these things, too, but who can go near to get them," he said to himself. "The most we can get out of Father Sun is the shots of light upon the Earth, through the air," he further reasoned. "These are the real jewels, the spirit-thoughts, body-thoughts, and material jewels of the Earth that the Great Mystery invested in her, and with which he adorned and decorated her," said Unktomi thoughtfully.

After due preparation, Miniwancakeya and his swarthy young companion were ready to enter the country of the sacred people. They went down a deep and vast valley surrounded by ranges of mountains with many cliffs and palisades along which were many, many caves, the homes of the Great Medicine Men of the nation.

As they proceeded, guided by the scouts, it became darker and darker, until as if they were in a deep forest in the night. They could scarcely see and know where they were going. At last the scouts stopped and told them to sit down, which they obeyed. After a time, lights all along the mountain sides and cliffs and the deep valley appeared like many campfires. Behold, they were in a beautiful country. Miniwancakeya and he were before the Council of the Great Medicine Chiefs. Strangely, they could feel, hear, and see everything that happened upon the Earth.

Miniwancakeya then told Unktomi that he must conduct himself properly, for these chiefs have the medicine of feeling knowledge. He further added, for the benefit of Unktomi, "This is to be so we too will have that power while we are under the Medicine Chiefs' influence and showing them the laws of the Sacred Ritual."

There sat before them the Council of Great Chiefs. This not only included representatives of the great confederation of the Toad-Turtle-Reptiles, but also many other representatives, such as Crabs and others. But none of the fish nations were there— they lived in the country above them.

When they had finished the feast and smoked the sacred pipe, the Great Sea Serpent spoke. He simply said,—"We have adopted them; since they have come so far for the knowledge of life, we will open to them some of the secrets of life which our mother has invested in us. We will instruct the chief, Miniwancakeya, in the medicines of life and the secrets of the Sacred Ritual. We will then initiate him and authorize him to teach the people above us the laws of the Ritual. But he must know that danger comes at the breaking of any of the laws of the Ritual. He must know that disobedience means destruction of a nation.

"We will first show him the powers in the Ritual and the Medicine."

The scouts were first sent out to announce to the world the event about to come. The great Water Drum was struck once. The whole water-world was at once astir—a deep resonant *A-ho-ho-ho-ho* reverberated throughout the world. After this, the water spirits, pushing the water into banks and columns, advanced one after another. As the drum struck in, the procession gradually increased; the whole world danced in the water, land, and air, for the Earth is dancing to a sacred drumbeat. The water, with war whoops, danced in great columns, while some went up in great masses into the air and danced with the air spirits, and in turn, the water spirits and the air spirits danced together in the water. Their war whoops, too, were terrible. Sometimes, in the excitement, the Earth herself shook like a leaf. When the Wet Drum is beaten softly, it is a gentle rain. At the end the *A-ho-ho-ho* was again heard, which died away in a deep murmur.

This, the Great Chief told Miniwancakeya, was the Sacred Medicine dance, and also it was called Mother Earth's dance, for it was the dance of nature and the elements, in which the water spirit and the air spirit dance (water and electricity dance). This is the great Meda-wa dance of the Indian religion: Medicine and

Masonic dance. During this dance, all creatures, water and land animals, go under cover and protection.

While the dance was going on, Unktomi looked up into the water-sky. Behold, the water-heaven was full of the people of every water-nation and tribe. Each class was seeking shelter under cliffs and high banks. Some were left on the prairie where there were heavy forests. Anywhere, anyhow, Unktomi and Miniwancakeya were given the sacred power of vision while they were there. This is why Unktomi saw all the people above him.

The Great Sea Serpent had said, "It is enough," and the dance was over.

The War Drum was used at this event, part of the time.

In this great dance of Nature, even inanimate trees, plants, grasses, all took part; even the little rain drops patted their little feet on the Mother Earth or on the shoulders of plants and animals.

When this dance was over, the great Medicine Feast began. After that, Miniwancakeya was initiated and instructed in secrets, healing medicine, and the laws of the Ritual. He alone was empowered to introduce the society among the upper water world and among the people of the surface world.

When all these things were carefully taught to Miniwancakeya, they returned to the land world. You will remember that Unktomi was not taught directly, nor was authority given him to spread the philosophy and the Sacred Ritual, because they knew his material mind could not be trusted.

"The next lesson is how Miniwancakeya organized societies among the upper world people, and how Unktomi claimed equal power with him, but failed," said Weyuha.

5

The Land Animals, the Sacred Ritual, and the World Contest for Speed

IN THE PILGRIMAGE OF MINIWANCAKEYA AND UNKTOMI TO the country of the Great Medicine Men and the autocrats of the animal people of the Earth, they knew that Miniwancakeya was representing them in seeking the sacred knowledge of the principles of life, and it was with this understanding Miniwancakeya went as the authorized messenger. Unktomi, to be sure, accompanied him, on his own responsibility, but was not duly appointed representative; therefore the Great Medicine Men did not receive him as such, and did not authorize him to teach the laws of the Sacred Ritual or to organize societies.

When the heralds of the tribes announced throughout the world the return of Miniwancakeya and Unktomi bringing the sacred knowledge, a great council was called. To this council all the people came. In this great council Miniwancakeya reported their experiences on the journey and what they found, and finally the great commission he had received and the Ritual which would guide them thenceforth. Here Unktomi tried to induce Miniwancakeya to say he was made the war chief of the world, but instead Miniwancakeya rebuked him for trying to amend the sacred commission. Thereupon, Unktomi reported that he was present when the sacred commission was given and therefore, he was entitled to something. The least he, Miniwancakeya, could do was to make him the keeper of the War Drum and the war totems. To this the old Medicine man replied,

"When I received the commission, I was enjoined to follow the Ritual and not politics. As you had accompanied me on the sacred journey, you may pound the Sacred War Drum when we come to demonstrate the war medicine," he told Unktomi.

Miniwancakeya explained everything concerning the Ritual and the Medicine bundles, which were contained in the sacred life-shell or snail. Then he also produced the war bundles and their totems and the two sacred drums. When all these were fully explained, he advised the people to prepare themselves by going into steam baths (sweat lodges) and fasting for four days; then the Medicine drum will be struck once, the forerunner of the world dance, the sacred dance, the dance of the Earth with her children throughout her dominion and sphere of influence. All these directions were faithfully obeyed and carried out.

So it came to pass, on a clear calm day, when the sun was bright and the sky was very blue, the Sacred Drum was heard. It had been ordered by Miniwancakeya to be struck gently; so it was done. It went over the whole Earth in a wave, and the Spirit began to move. The sky dropped a curtain of blanket. The water began to swell in columns and advanced; the whispered songs were heard; the grass and trees began to dance, while from heaven above waters came down dancing. As the Sacred Drum was struck softer, the excitement of the dance of the animals became freer. There was a gentle rain. When the striking of the Sacred Wet Drum ceased and the spirits of the sky departed, the blanket was removed. The sky assumed its blue. Then the feast began, eating the sacred food.

After a recess, Miniwancakeya again announced that the sacred war bundle will be opened. All the attending ceremonies were carefully carried out. Then it was that Miniwancakeya ordered Unktomi to officiate at the War Drum. The enthusiast was so glad because at last he was recognized, he struck the drum a heavy blow, and the result was a thunder clash. As he continued the blows, the world was involved instantly in a terrible rain storm, with deafening war whoops that shook the mountains, and the waters arose in mountainous waves, while the trees were uprooted and the rocks were chasing each other from the hillsides. When he stopped, the spirit warrior swept away everything and the people were frantically fleeing in every direction for protection. The deep reverberating *A-ho-ho-ho . . . ho* came from the depth of the Big Water, as a protest and a warning. Miniwancakeya rebuked Unktomi for his unwise act. "Ah, my good and great Medicine man, it is best to let these ignorant and boastful people know what power lurks in these bundles," he replied. Because of this act, Unktomi was never thereafter allowed to handle the sacred things, although he boasts he can work them as well as Miniwancakeya.

Now the laws and the medicines governing the physical life were thus brought about, and all the animals eventually conformed to them by teachings of Miniwancakeya. In this work he in turn authorized and commissioned leaders among all the animal people of the Earth, to organize societies and teach their respective tribes the laws of the ritual of the Sacred Bundles, which will guide them henceforth.

The Toad-Turtle-Reptile nations were appointed as the seers, although the other animal tribes were entrusted with portions of the Ritual, such customs and laws as concern hunting and warfare within the dominion and sphere of their Mother. Some of these were amended by the influence of the Father, the Sun.

My children, do not confuse in your mind the things which come from the Great Spirit and the things with which he endowed the Earth.

You must bear in mind that the laws of the Great Mystery are not changeable, for they are constant. The things of the Earth and the Sun occasionally readjust themselves like a person changes steps in walking, or positions in sitting or lying down. But in such a change, the whole world is made to feel the force of it. Sometimes it is a disaster and calamity to the children of the Earth. When the Sun's influence comes into hers, the excitement and enthusiasm causes all the storms, rains, or sunshine, and also the cold and the heat, which are very important to physical life. All these were embodied in the laws of the Sacred Ritual. Miniwancakeya had been wisely informed that some of these powers were held by the element spirits, to take charge of the air country, as also they did with the water and the land spirits of their country, according to the principles and laws of the Ritual. In each region there were Spirit beings commissioned to control. To them one may appeal for physical aid or benefit, under certain rules, as set forth in the teaching of the Ritual. Through the authorized or commissioned bodies, animate or inanimate, a worthy being may see visions of his or his people's future or events which concern them. That is why our people practice the custom of fasting, to get themselves into pure spiritual attitude.

It was also given in the Ritual that one may appeal directly to the Earth or the Sun Spirit for physical help. But the Spirit or Soul Prayer, that is, the prayer for the spirit, must directly go to the Great Spirit, but not for petty or selfish physical things. No words must be used in prayers, for that will insult the intelligence of the Spirits, especially in the Spirit Prayer. Chants or dirges without words may be used, for that is like a child's grief or yearning sobs. It is not necessary for me to go into detail at this time, because when man is created, these are again taken up, but because it was here where these customs began, I want you to understand now, so that it will come clearer when you study the man and his relationship to these matters.

Unktomi had been expelled from the order. He was intelligent and a clever reasoner, a logician, but he was not very spiritual and was prone to use everything for selfish trickery and personal advancement. He catered to politics all his life.

The people of the Earth now were well established by the laws of the Ritual, and orders were well maintained among them. There were rivalries between all the nations in physical sports. Something like party strife; each tribe showing how skillful they were in running, swimming, and flying. These contests between tribes had often brought many nations together to see the affair. Sometimes they were much excited, but their laws and customs were well established, which kept them within their sense of justice and honor. Often times they have disputes, but these are always adjusted in friendly ways. In most of these bad feelings, it turns out to be Unktomi was the cause, but being so intelligent, he skillfully and shrewdly kept himself well concealed in the background. If there was a possibility of exposing him, he cleverly put on other causes, or he would argue them out of it. In this way, he caused all the troubles between the tribes, which eventually became customary with them.

The first one of the important difficulties of the water people and the land animals came about by his tricks in the world contest for speed. All the water people (mostly the fish) were one party against all the creatures of the land, for a race around the world (Earth). In this, too, he was the instigator and the exciting cause of the event, for he was an adventurist and gambler, always looking about for something in which to advertise himself.

In the race, openly he was neutral, but on the sly he was coaching the land animals, claiming he was one of them. First, he had the neutral animals ruled out. That included all creatures who lived part time in water and land, but from among them he selected the judges of the race: the Elephant, the Whale, the Beaver, the Big Turtle, and the Swan. All the waterfowls were excluded.

The race was a string knot race (relay race) in which one member from each tribe of the two great nations was chosen. The wager was, the winners will be considered thereafter superior to the other nations. They paired off according to their speed. I will tell you the names of the beginners and the finishers of the race. The Trout against the Cliff Swallow started the race, and the Crab and the Land Turtle were at the finish. Some of you have heard this legend of the world race. I tell it now, because of the trouble it made.

Unktomi had coached some of the land runners to deceive the fish, and, I am sorry to say, these listened to him and were dishonest. First place, Unktomi got them to ask the fish for concessions, on account of the mountains, saying that the fish had a level track, while the land animals had to climb mountains, and other disadvantages, which the judges allowed. Then Unktomi got the little Prairie Owl to play dishonest. When his turn was reached, he may start in good faith but soon drop behind his opponent, the Sword Fish. And when he reached a bush he there hid himself, while his twin brother, who was waiting in concealment near the end of his course, jumps and starts from there as soon as his brother hides. In this way he reaches the next runner before the Sword Fish was half way on the course. He had also bribed the Crow, the Magpie, the Blue Heron, the Land Lizard, and several other slow runners. Of course, the fish could do that, too, but there was no Unktomi to teach them dishonesty.

The last lap of the course was closely watched. The people were in intense excitement and breathlessly looked on, as the Land Turtle and the Crab finished the race.

Unktomi had the chief Wolf protest that young man Crab did not race fair. He pointed out to the judges that Crab had run first frontward, but when he was winded he changed front to backwards. This seemed to him very unfair. As a result, he won only by his tail. Unktomi claimed for the animals, if he had run as he had started, front forward, he would have lost the race.

The judges, Swan, Beaver, and Big Turtle, declared this protest was well taken, and young man Crab was ruled out. The Whale and the Elephant said that it was natural for Crab to run either way, but the other judges insisted it was against the rule, so they yielded. The land animals won by default; all the nations of the water protested. This resulted in a war between them, which has gone on ever since, and they have never admitted that the land animals are superior to them to this day.

In this way, Unktomi started all the difficulties and warfare among all the animals of the Earth.

The legends of their struggles against one another are many, but that is the business of the parents to teach. Therefore I leave them out, except when it comes strong in the main legend of the animal and is a link in the customs of the man and the animal.

Weyuha again discharged his pupils with these words of advice: My good children, we will not now take up the coming of the child, our great-great-grandparent. I want you to be very careful in mastering what I have told you, for that will help you to understand the laws of the man's life.

6

The Coming of Eshnaicage,
the Spirit Messenger

I TOLD YOU WHEN YOU FINISHED LISTENING TO THE STORY
of Miniwancakeya and Unktomi going to the bottom of the
Big Water to secure the Sacred Ritual that we would take up
the coming of the Child who was to be the parent of the Man-
race, the Man-people. It is very important that we should know
what took place in preparation to his coming. I want you to
remember well that this event in this story is not the work of the
Sacred Ritual, nor was it brought about by the Great Medicine
Men of the Earth. It seems to have come by order of the Great
Mystery Himself. To be sure, all the elements were in it, and the
Great Sacred Drum was sounded; yet it was understood that
the Great Mystery Himself had it to be done.

It was a beautiful, bright summer day, and Mother Earth
was wearing her beautiful, many-colored summer clothing. Her
children all over the world were apparently happy and in peace.

The Great Sacred Wet Drum of the Great Medicine people, down in the depth of the Big Water, was heard. Indeed, it
rumbled down in the bowels of the mountains. At first, being so
gentle, the people of the Earth gave no heed, except as a sign for
one of the usual dances of the Earth Children. In a little while
however, the water and the air spirits were in a war council. At
this instant, the National Scout, Cliff Swallow, was sent out by
the Great Medicine Men of the Deep. He was spreading the

news that the Great Mystery was dissatisfied with the children of the Earth.

Chief Swallow had directed every herald of all the tribes to make haste to inform their people of the impending celebration of the elements, as signaled by the Sacred Wet Drum. This caused much thinking and subdued excitement among all the tribes of the Earth. They seemed to feel a calamity was about to come upon them. While the people were in this state of excitement and prayer, Unktomi appeared among them. He tried every way to find out what the excitement was all about, but no one was willing to tell him. They feared the Great Mystery might be further offended.

His keen observation soon convinced him that there was something serious and unusual about to come. He went about, ears and eyes open. He was rewarded by hearing the whispered talk between the Badger and the Ground Hog. They were talking about where would be a safe place for their children to go during the approaching danger, when all the elements were to dance and celebrate the coming of the Spirit Messenger from the Great, Great Spirit.

"What did you say?" asked Unktomi eagerly.

"Oh, it's nothing. We were just talking about safe homes for our children to go to, when the Wet Drum is sounded again," they replied.

"Ah, you must not conceal anything from your patient and faithful friend. I know what you said. I knew for a long while of this. Repeat what you have said; I want to know if you are honest."

So thus, cunningly, he got the Badger and the Ground Hog to repeat what they really had said. "That's right, you are honest," he told them. He himself had told a falsehood in getting them to repeat what they had said. In this way, he found out the coming of the messenger from the Great Spirit, Eshnaicage, who is superior to the Sun and the Earth. Unktomi went forth among the different tribes, telling them to prepare themselves to receive the Spirit Messenger from the Great Spirit. He did this to make them think that he was authorized by the Spirit.

The animals of the Earth were not fully prepared when the Wet Drum was sounded heavier and louder, and its progress brought the Spirit elements, who took possession of the air, water, and land. The war whoops were terrible; even Mother Earth was in a tremble, while the Sun hid his face. The sea was torn up and thrown into a series of mountainous waves, and some of the little lands in mid-sea were torn up into splinters and set afire on their fragments, which can be seen afar in the night, and continued to burn after the storm of the Spirits. Great bodies of the water from the Big Water were carried up into the sky prairies as prisoners. These, when freed, fled back to the Earth in haste, to the nearest point, thence on land returned to the Big Water. We can see their trails yet, some of them still in use by them in lesser celebrations.

In spite of the warnings and preparations, many creatures lost their lives, both in water and land. This great celebration left Mother Earth with many more wrinkles, because of their rough action upon her body. There were not only wrinkles of every size, but also large depressions. The former we called the Big Rivers, the streams, and the brooklets. The deep depressions were called valleys and plains and lakes of every size. The storm had swept away all the plants and trees.

All this was fully related in our folklore. It is related in the lore of the Legend that this kind of calamity happened three times in the life of the Earth, thus far. Twice it happened as it is given here, and once it was attended by heavy snow; the world was buried in white snow.

In each case, the animals were nearly all destroyed by water, snow, or by starvation, and at each time, many of the creatures were not allowed to be born in the same form again. In others, their privileges were limited or denied them. But each of these world events have their own legends; therefore it is put in here only briefly.

It seems these events took quite a long time, and the time between them was ages. This one was the first; the other two came about in the life of the man. It is said that these events were brought about by the conduct and behavior of the inhabitants of the Earth. First cause was—too great a population; second was war against the man; third, they became headstrong and obnoxious and lost in their own doings, and disobeyed the laws of the body and the spirit—the Ritual.

When the Spirits stopped their celebration, it took some time for the waters to return to their home. All the waters which were held prisoners on the land had gradually returned to the Big Water, and what was left of the animals returned to their roaming places, but there was little food for them to eat. Then it was that Mother Earth and Father Sun planted seeds and brought forth many vegetables, seeds, and fruits for their starving children. In due time—a long time—the world was beautiful again.

I forgot to tell you how Unktomi said he saved himself, in the great carnage.

When it was possible for anyone to come out of his hiding place, Unktomi came out in the open to view the wreckage. As he was running along the shores of the water, he came upon a turtle. "How, how, Brother," he addressed him, but the turtle, being worn out and half starved, did not raise his head to look at him. "Cheer up, cheer up, Brother; the worst is over," continued Unktomi.

"Ugh," said the dejected turtle, "There is nothing to cheer up for; I have lost all my children."

"Ah, ah. That is where I have the advantage of you. You see, I have no children. If I have any, I do not recognize them; they came without my permission; therefore, I let them go to hunt for themselves, just as I do. Cheer up, you have lived through an experience that ought to comfort and make you wise," he added.

"But there is no life or comfort when one is deep in sorrow," said the turtle.

"Ah, ah. You forget that life is made up of sorrows and happiness, sometimes badly mixed to be sure. That is the soil of wisdom; that is where wisdom grows," he curtly declared.

"And how did you save yourself?" the turtle asked.

"Oh, Brother Turtle, it was a narrow escape. I would never want another such experience in the rest of my life," he replied. "Fortunately, I found out what was to come to the Earth people, through Brother Badger and Ground Hog. I at once started for the mountain, but it was too late. The celebration, as they called it (I would say a desperate battle), had begun. I tried to get into two or three different caves on the mountainside, but each time, before I was safely in, the wind warriors dragged me out and threw me down on the outside. I got among the trees, but those, too, were torn up by the roots. I got down on the plains, where I was picked up by a mountain stream. Soon I was on the way to the Big Water, carried by the rivers. There I was tossed unmercifully, this way and that way; between times, I was shot up into the air to great heights. I had just a little life left in me when I saw a Sea Snail, which was shot up from the bottom of the Big Water. I caught his nose and shouted to him in the midst of the roaring and boiling water. I said to him, 'Let me in, Brother Snail. I have plenty of food which you may share with me until the end of this warfare!' He listened, and before he knew it I was inside his house. I said to him, 'Let's go down to the bottom of the Big Water and find some cave; we will hide there; they cannot get us there, unless they should grind up Mother Earth.' That was where we were until today, when he let me out. I will tell you, he is the most religious person I ever knew. His house was full of music, too. But, I confess to you, I lied to him when I said I had much food. However, that is what happens when one is closely chased," said Unktomi.

The great mother, the Earth, was in this manner washed and cleaned. Of the great burden of feeding so many thankless children, she was relieved. In due time, she had rested and regained her health, which made her spirit happy, and her body was handsome and graceful again.

One day the Wet Drum was heard, but it was soft and gentle. There was a gentle warm rain; as it stopped, the Sun came out in his full regalia. The children of the Earth were very happy. The Cliff Swallow Scout had been sent out, inviting all the people to a great council. When they all came and settled in their assigned places, their parents, the Sun and the Earth, addressed them. They said they had lived for their children, but many of them became unruly; therefore, the Great Spirit was dissatisfied. The result was the punishment. "Now, only a few of you we have saved. The Great Spirit sent you a Spirit Messenger. He has come."

Out of the great blue sky, a white cloud floated over their heads, and, although there was a clear sky, from it came a flash of lightning. It struck the Earth, and there stood before them a noble and handsome young man. *A-ho-ho-ho-ho!* was the deep murmuring sound from the sky.

"It is His will," he said, "that I come." The children of the

Earth bowed their heads in reverence. "That you may be more kindly in your conduct toward one another, I come to see what is needed to make your mother and father happy, for that will please the Great Spirit. You must try again," he said.

Thus Eshnaicage, the Great Teacher, creator of the human child, came.

7

The Creation and Nurture of Waceheska, the First Human Baby

MY GOOD CHILDREN, WE HAVE LISTENED TO THE LEGEND of the Earth-Sun children and their troubles. We now come to a new situation. The Great Teacher, the Creator of our great-grandfather, the man, has come.

A new race is coming, by the creation of the little baby man. Remember, my children, before this time the creatures who inhabited the Earth were called the animal people. They were our forerunners, our relatives, because our great-grandmother comes from them. She was therefore longer on Earth than the man. Her spirit is the same as his spirit—both come from the Great Spirit. She came through Nature; he came direct from the Spirit, therefore he has the seed. She came in this manner so that she may give the body to the spirit. But it will all come clear to you when you hear how all these things came about. The spirit enters the body which is nature, but this work took some time, as you will learn. You must observe the reasons given for every step of the progress of Nature and the animals toward the final man. The child was a spirit; Eshnaicage gave it a body form. But let the Legend tell you.

When Eshnaicage made himself known that he will be their brother, and was seeking to establish for them a condition in which they may develop and live in an intelligent way, also to understand better the meaning of the Sacred Ritual, they became satisfied and content to try to follow the laws of the Ritual.

They had learned that the new teacher is powerful, because he hears even a whisper, anywhere on Earth, and understands their minds better than they do themselves. Yet he was willing to adapt himself to their conditions, so that he may sympathize with them in every way. Therefore he desired to adopt their body (material) life. Furthermore, he will not, himself, do them any harm. It was to be the laws which will react on them when they disobey. He came to readjust their customs.

In this way they got accustomed to him, but they were very careful what they said or did while he was among them. There were not so many of them, because the storm had destroyed most of the people. In fact, many of the tribes were entirely wiped out. This is true of the more obnoxious and defying kind. Another reason was, when the human spirit child is created, they will not be there to bother him. So the world was readjusted once more, and all things seemed to be in a proper and peaceful state, because there was much food and much country for them to roam in, without any fear of causing trouble.

The animal people guardedly discussed among themselves the character and work of the new teacher, in which Unktomi was always the disturbing mind. He was very careful not to offend Eshnaicage. Indeed, he tried to impress the people that he upheld all his teachings, and that he is the intimate friend of the Great Teacher; at the same time, he raises questions in respect to the very philosophy he came to establish. Often times he said, "It is all for good, but I cannot help feeling that this sort of teaching may lead us to servitude. It looks to me as though too much obedience will lead us to serve some other race."

He was reprimanded by the wise members of the tribes. "Such thoughts will cause difficulties in a happy family," they declared.

He replied, "I was only expressing possibilities."

All was well with the people, for their relations with their teacher were cordial, and their progress was harmonious and peaceful while Eshnaicage lived thus among them, with the understanding that he was their Sacred Teacher. Therefore, even the great and wise Medicine Men, down in the bottom of the Big Water, were very careful in following his teachings of the Sacred Ritual.

During this time, the people, although fearing and respecting him, watched critically everything he said and did in order to understand and follow his wishes. But Unktomi, at every opportunity, puts in a disturbing question or an idea which confuses them, for which he was always cautioned and complained of, and sometimes even reprimanded, by the Medicine Men.

Unktomi had appeared at a social smoking of old men, as usual, full of humor and witty remarks. He sat down among them with the remark, "I feel like an old man who has worried himself into sleeplessness, because his good advices were not heeded. At such times and feelings, nothing is more welcome than a good smoke," he declared. "By the way, Brother Wolf, you are always on the scout for your people; have you heard or seen Eshnaicage lately?"

"No, I have not. It is true I have traversed the country, back and forth, very thoroughly."

"Brother Antelope, have you seen him?" he further asked the swift-footed antelope. "It seems strange that nobody has seen him for a long time," he observed. "He could not be sick, for he has very good medicine," he added. "I was wondering if he is not up to something serious. I think of this because Brother Badger told me, the last time he saw him, he was up on the highest mountain and appeared to him strangely, in deep thought, and acted queer. Perhaps he is getting tired of our way of living," he further remarked.

While these old men and Unktomi were exchanging thoughts, there came Chief Eagle. "Ah, ah, Chief Eagle! You have come when we needed just such chief as you," the ready and alert politician addressed and welcomed him.

"Brothers, I have come on a very important errand. Eshnaicage has sent me to tell the people of the world to attend his council. He desires we should send a tribe's messenger to all the nations with the news of the council call," he told them.

"What is the object of the council? The people of the world are in peace," inquired Unktomi.

Thereupon the Eagle messenger replied, "He has a strange and wonderful child in his teepee, and for this reason he wishes to meet the people of the world in council," he told them, and departed.

Eshnaicage had withdrawn from the people for a period of time. No one had noticed, but the restless and active mind of the world's politician had again called the attention of the people to the fact. It had come to Eshnaicage's mind, and occupied it for some time, that the study and survey of the life of the animal people had convinced him that the time had come to bring forth the man-child who will rule the world. In his teepee, which was pitched in the center of the Earth, he had been in prayer for months, and that was when Unktomi missed him.

At last, the Spirit sounded the sacred *A-ho-ho-ho!* Then it was that Eshnaicage made, out of a cedar wood, a perfect little (tiny) man. He took some of his own blood, with which he painted it and threw it through the smoke hole of his teepee. It rolled on the wall of the teepee down to the Earth. He heard the deep *A-ho-ho-ho!* as it struck the ground.

In a little while, he heard a baby cry. Eshnaicage came out of his teepee and found the tiny baby, big as a seed, but it was a perfect little human being. He took it in his hand and said, "Thou shall be my little brother."

The Great Teacher had prepared already an Ene-teepee (sweat lodge) nearby, to which he took the tiny living creature. He kept it in there for a long time. When he took it out, the tiny living thing became as big as a baby bird. Then he called Chief Eagle and the Swan to bring their wives to him. The Eagle and Swan Women made the first cradle for the child; but the inside lining of down was later arranged by the Humming Bird and Oriole young women. The outside was embroidered by the Porcupine Woman with her quills.

When these had been carefully arranged, he sent out the Eagle Chief to announce the great council. At the council, he told them that the father of another race was brought upon the Earth. They must help him in raising the child. He must have their blood. Therefore, the mothers must take turns in nursing the child, and they must love him and take care of him, as if it was their own child. He entrusted them with this obligation and told them to be faithful and patient with him. The animal people pledged themselves to obey Eshnaicage to do anything for the child, even to sacrificing themselves.

When all these matters were settled, Unktomi got up, putting on all the innocent and imploring manner of which he is capable, and asked Eshnaicage, would he be pleased to allow the poor and humble public to view and examine the child.

The Great Teacher knew the character of Unktomi, but the request was proper, so he granted the request, as it was his purpose to have them know the child, and in turn, when he grew up, he must know every one of them. "For," he said, "you are brothers in the spirit—you all come from the Great Spirit, only differing in body, form, color, and habits. To that extent also, in thinking and manner of locomotion or transportation, and you are all born of the Earth and the Sun, as regards your bodies, but he comes direct from the Spirit, and it is our work to give him the body. In due time he will be adjusted in body and mind as it should be. I am sent to watch and guide his growth, but you have the opportunity to help in making him understand you and the Earth-Sun laws."

These explanations of Eshnaicage's were received by all the animals and they agreed to abide by them and carry them out. They were permitted to examine the child.

"Whough!" said Loon Woman. "He has little feet shaped like my children."

"Yes, but look at the nose of your children. He has not a sign of a sharp long bill," said the Swan Woman. "At least he is as handsome as my children," she added with some pride. The waterfowls were the first to examine the little child.

"It is too early to show any feathers on its body," observed the Goose Mother.

Medicine Woman Owl was the next to come, with much pomp and confidence. She examined it thoroughly from head to foot. "There are no signs of feet and claws, but surely he has eyes like ours," she declared.

And so, all the different tribes in succession examined it with the hope they might find some resemblance to their tribe. After all the bird and fish tribes had had their turn came the land animals. It was the women representatives of the tribes who made the examinations.

The Buffalo women discovered the child had a head and fur on it like theirs, but the Wolf Mother contradicted by saying, "The child certainly has no feet with hooves."

Old Badger Woman simply remarked that it was too young to show any marked resemblance, but ventured to add that her children were much like him when they were born.

It was then, the big Grizzly Bear Woman brushed everyone aside and took the child in her arms. "Behold," she said, "he is as naked as my own babe bear when it was born. See his little feet and hands—they are exactly like my babe."

"Ugh," replied Porcupine Woman, "my babe when it came looked just like him."

And even the Mouse Woman claimed some resemblance to her babes, in which the Grizzly reproached her, saying, "Do you suppose this beautiful child lives in the meadows, shut out from the world? It can only resemble people who have a high station in life," she declared with emphasis.

This ended the viewing of the little man-child.

Eshnaicage appointed a number of leading mothers to oversee the manner in which the child must be taken care of. Chief Eagle Woman, Medicine woman; Grizzly Woman for doctoring; Chief Swan Woman for comfort; under her, many birds and ducks, for nursery, and Grizzly Woman had animals of their tribe to help. They engaged, under Mother Meadow Lark, many nursery singers of all the birds, to soothe and comfort the child. Owl Woman was assistant to the Grizzly, in doctoring the child. Many of the animals brought to the child food, as he grew older and could eat other food. The squirrels and mice and the like were good in providing delicate foods.

But at the start, the committee of women of which Chief Eagle Woman was the head, had no end of difficult problems, in reference to the women selected from each tribe to nurse the child. Unktomi had said to them, "You good women will have to get Eshnaicage to provide a long pipe (hose) for the little child to reach the breast of some of the big women, and those who live way down in the water. It would be too bad to have the child lose their milk on this account, because their milk is the strongest."

To this, the Turtle Woman replied, "Unktomi, you need not think you were the first to discover that, for we have already brought that matter before Eshnaicage. He has arranged with all the mothers down there, to send their milk by their next neighbors until it reaches those who live both in water and on land."

"Ugh," exclaimed Unktomi, "It will all be sour before it gets to the child."

"No," they replied, "They drink it and pass it on to the next."

"Ah, ah. He will be a great half breed, for he will be nursed by everybody—no one will know from his traits, who is his real parent," curtly remarked the shrewd logician.

"But it is the wish of Eshnaicage; he ought to know what is good for the child," said Chief Eagle Woman. "Besides, the food which we eat does not affect the spirit," she added.

"But the body and the spirit together must influence each other," retorted Unktomi.

While the child was growing, the women were constantly watching it, hoping he might grow into one of the many tribes. When, for instance, he got his teeth, the Buffalo Woman said, "He has some teeth in the lower jaw like ours, but he also has them on the upper, where we have none." The Wolf and Bear classes rejoiced, because theirs were similar to his. But when he began to move on all fours, they were wild with joy, for he surely resembled them, they thought; but they were so disappointed when he walked off on two legs. Thus he grew before the eyes of the people.

There was some trouble among the women of the different tribes. I will only tell you of one, in which Unktomi was accused of the trouble, and was tried by the wise men of the nations before Eshnaicage. But this is a long lesson, and you are tired. Besides, this trial of Unktomi is important, as it brought forth something which became a world custom.

I will stop here. We will have the trial next.

8

Unktomi's Trial

IT IS OUR PRIVILEGE TO KNOW THAT THE CHILD WAS NOW
thus provided with his keeping, and with as much comfort as
the mothers of the world could give. Eshnaicage's purpose was
to create in them not only an individual, but a tribal interest in
the child, a pride in their share of developing him. On the other
hand, the child would become conscious of the obligation he
owes to these mothers. Then, too, he and their children must
have a feeling of brotherhood, for being nursed by the same
mothers.

Thus the work of raising the child, and its cares, seemed to
have progressed in a well-ordered way. But just like all other
human or animal affairs, they soon came to some unlooked-for
troubles.

Unktomi had been very observing with a critical mind. He
had heard Eshnaicage to say he "desired to have every mother
or representative from every tribe, to share in the nursing, the
care, and the teaching of the child, just as he himself will do
everything for the child's welfare and its education." With these
ideas in mind, Unktomi daily visited the nursery to keep himself
informed of all that went on there.

He soon discovered that the women of the little tribes such
as the Ants, Mosquitoes, Flies, in fact all the insect tribes, were
discriminated against by the bird women. His shrewd political
mind was alert to seize this obvious discrimination. "Ah, ah,
here is an opening for me to be a hero of these people," he said

to himself. He did not hesitate to praise the work of the women. He was therefore very well acquainted with the inside doings of the mothers.

He watched for an opportunity to point out this fact and set it before the minds of the disadvantaged little mothers. At last the opportunity came.

Unktomi was sitting before a council of the little mothers, pompously and complacently filling his long-stemmed pipe. He had managed to bring about this council by some of his associates, but to have it appear the women themselves called it. It was their indignation council. "Ah! You know, good friends, it has been my principle to correct the wrongs that one of the tribes committed against another. Indeed, I think I was born a peacemaker," he boasted, to lead their minds, and to excite them. "I understand you have been shamefully discriminated against in the work of providing milk for Eshnaicage's baby brother, and this meeting is to decide how to make a complaint to him, and you have asked me to advise you. Let me hear first, what are the truths and basis of your complaints, and how it all came about?" Thus he cunningly coaxed and led them.

Young and beautiful Mother Fly nervously and shyly got up and said, "Oh, friend Unktomi, we have been very careful and faithful to the child's needs and comforts. But when it was our turn to nurse the child, Chief Eagle Woman, Swan, and the Swallow were snobbish, and hurried us, even to cut our time short. Therefore the little child did not get enough milk, and being deprived of his food and hungry, he would cry for more. Then they would blame us for it. Furthermore they would say we have no milk, or else, it is not good."

It was then that the Mosquito Mother arose and denounced all the bird tribes, saying, "They think they are cleaner and more refined, and that we are unclean and irritating the child, so it cries when we take charge. We are the cleanest people in the world. We eat clean juice of everything, and we can raise more children in one year than they could in their whole life. This shows we have good milk and plenty of it. Our clothing is clean and we are a brave race. We raise more brave warriors in one family than their whole tribe can raise. Besides, our men are great hunters. Also, we are a race of singers; the world hears our songs." So the complaint was one voice among all the women of the little insects.

"How, how, women; no one can blame you for making a complaint to Eshnaicage. He is honest; he will listen to you. He should reprimand Eagle Woman and her associates, for their unjust conduct toward your people."

They appointed young Mother Bee and Mother Woodtick to present their grievances. Mother Bee has a sweet voice and a sugar tongue, and Mother Woodtick is a woman of few words; she will not spoil Mother Bee's sweet speech. All she would say will be, "It is true."

"You have made a good selection in these two women to call upon Eshnaicage," commented Unktomi.

When Eshnaicage called into the council the women who had charge of the child, there was an outcry of all the bird tribes, which could be heard all over the Earth. "Shame, shame!" declared the Eagle women.

"It is no surprise to me," said the Swan Woman. "It has been rumored that Unktomi is up to some mischief with the excitable little people." It was only recently that the pretty Mother Humming Bird had heard said that the irrepressible Mosquito Mother boastfully declared to the Ant Mother that Unktomi had told them Eshnaicage will make the snobbish proud Eagle Woman be sorry for discriminating against the little mothers. They had appointed the Bee Woman and the Woodtick Mother to make the complaint to Eshnaicage. "It is a shame, Unktomi should again cause this trouble," declared the indignant Mother Swan.

The Loon Mother spoke up and suggested that Unktomi should be charged with disturbing the peace by propaganda and inciting one tribe against another. So the Loon Woman and the Owl Woman were appointed to make the formal charge against Unktomi to Eshnaicage.

Eshnaicage had patiently listened to the women parties on both sides, which resulted in the trial of Unktomi. He had many trials in his career with the animals, but I relate only this one which comes in the Legend of Creation.

Unktomi's Trial

When Eshnaicage reviewed the charges, he came to the conclusion that it will be a lesson to both parties. So he ordered the trial. From the neutral tribes, he had appointed the judges, speakers, and the men to keep order, while he acted as a referee. For, he decided, they should try him according to their established customs and their understanding of justice; he only wanted to see a fair play. It was a dispute between the bird people and the insect tribes.

They appointed Unktehe, the chief of the Ritual Keepers, for he knows all the laws of the Sacred Ritual, to preside over the trial. The Sachems, from the various Toad-Turtle-Reptile tribes, were the judges, while from all the animal (big) tribes, they had warriors to keep order. This has become a custom of the Indians from that far-off time to this day.

These were the Sachems (judges): the Rattle Snake, the Big Lake Turtle, the Land Lizard, the Alligator, and the Big Toad. The Grizzly Bear, the Tiger, the Buffalo, the Wolf, the Elk, and the Moose were the big warriors to keep order during the trial. The Coyote, the Red Fox, the Bobtail Cat, the Lynx, and the Wolverine were the special second-line police warriors, while the Antelope, the Deer and Caribou, and the Reindeer were the messengers. The Bull Frog was the herald—the caller and announcer, all in one. Each of the contending parties selected their speakers. The bird people appointed the Sandhill Crane, with resonant voice; the Raven, with deep dignified voice; the Northern Goose, with a varying and pleasant voice; and the Redheaded Woodpecker.

Unktomi selected his speakers: the Bumblebee, the Dragonfly, and the Locust were his choice. "They are the most eloquent of all the orators," he said with much show of satisfaction. Eshnaicage was announced as he ascended his high position by the herald, Bull Frog, with heavy, deep voice. All the animals uttered a deep-sounding *A-ho-ho-ho!* Then Unktehe was announced, the people of the Earth were now in council.

There was not a grass blade, tree branch, or space on the ground unoccupied. All had been taken by the people or the spectators, and everything was in a breathless silence when Unktomi, the accused, came in with the guards, the warriors Grizzly and Tiger, on either side. He was tall, swarthy, and ungainly in body. He had a sweetgrass band around his heavy mass of hair. He wore no shirt, only a woven bullrush breech clout, suspended with a string of inner bark of basswood; a fern like a feather, stuck onto the back of his head. He had in one hand a long-stemmed pipe and a tobacco pouch; in the other, a palm fan. He had no leggings—only a pair of sandals.

When he entered, everybody craned and turned their necks to look at him. He gave one of his fascinating smiles. Then he held up both hands, with great reverence, toward Eshnaicage, and made a low bow. Next he held up one hand toward Unktehe, the presiding Medicine man, and to the Sachems. After that, he swept his hand over the great gathering and took his seat with his speakers.

When the great Unktehe got up with great difficulty, for he was thousands of winters old, the first thing he did was to ask the doorkeepers of the big arbor-court to have the doors closed. It had four entrances, and there were four doorkeepers, namely, the warriors Skunk, Little Centipede, Wasp, and Porcupine, to keep undesirables out. Then with much solemnity, he struck gently the small Wet Drum and shook the hoof rattle. This opened the Court.

The speaker, Sandhill Crane, got up and stretched his long legs and neck, then stepped into the circle in a very slow and dignified way. After a solemn pause, he said, "Oh, great and reverent Eshnaicage, within thy hearing and sight we have come to settle the charges brought by my race, the bird people, against Unktomi. It is our prayer and desire to be honest, and by truths prove the charges."

Then he turned to the aged Unktehe, addressing him thus, "In thy presence, with thy wisdom and great mind, inspire us to tell the truth and nothing but the truth. With thy permission, I state the charges of my people. Unktomi has brought dissension and discord among the women of the bird people and the insect race, in connection with the care of the infant child whom the Great Chief Spirit, Eshnaicage, has given to the people of the world."

A murmuring of *A-ho-ho-ho!* was uttered among the people. Then Unktehe commanded the bird people to bring their witnesses.

"Oh, ye judges, with your permission I present Chief Eagle Woman to tell what she knows of the management of the child," requested the speaker, Chief Sandhill Crane.

Chief Eagle Woman held her uplifted hand to Eshnaicage first, then to Unktehe. "The people of the world know that the Spirit Eshnaicage appointed me to take charge of the man-child which he created. It was his wish to have a mother from every tribe to share in the raising of the child. I have appointed Chief Swan Woman and others to see that proper and clean mothers from all the tribes be selected. They were in turn given the time to nurse, feed, and take care, and to comfort the child. All the mothers from the different tribes have patiently and faithfully performed their duties, although sometimes with much inconvenience, and sometimes, some sacrifices. But the manners and customs of some have caused much annoyance and discomfort to the child," she stated.

"You have always been fair and unbiased to all the mothers, have you not?" asked Chief Sandhill Crane.

"Yes," she replied.

"Do you know if there were any difficulties among the mothers of the different tribes in this work?"

"Lately, there have been," she replied.

"Do you know of any particular mother who is the cause of the trouble?"

"No, not personally."

"Do you know any person or persons, outside of the mothers, who made any trouble?"

"No, only hearsay."

It was then Chief Bumblebee, Unktomi's chief speaker, asked Chief Eagle Woman these questions, with permission of the Sachems.

Bumblebee: "Chief Eagle Woman, you say there are difficulties among the mothers from different tribes who nursed and took care of the man-child; what is the nature of the difficulties, and can you give an example?"

"I cannot," she replied.

"Why not?" Bumblebee asked.

"I did not hear or see them in dispute."

"Then how do you know there were any difficulties?"

"I heard my assistant talk about it."

"Then it is only rumor, as far as you know. Is it not?"

"Yes," she replied.

Bumblebee: "Is it not true there was no trouble, only a rumor, as far as you know?"

"Yes," she again replied.

"You have admitted in your statement that there was no one outside of the mothers who nursed and took care of the child; then who caused, incited, or led these mothers into any trouble or dissension?"

"I do not know," she answered.

Bumblebee said, "That is all."

Sandhill Crane then asked Eagle Woman this question: "Is it not a fact and generally known among all the women who had charge of the man-child, that Unktomi was the real cause of their trouble?"

"Yes," she replied.

At this instant, Unktomi poked Bumblebee in the ribs and whispered in his ear, "She has just denied that; she said, 'I know no one outside of the mothers who has caused any trouble among them.'"

So Bumblebee jumped up, saying, "Now, Eagle Woman, you have just admitted that no outsider had made or brought any trouble to these mothers. Remember the forked-tongued person's position in the world. Is it not true, you meant to say there were rumors among the women, but not proven?"

"Yes," she replied.

"That is all." He sat down with a triumphant air. Unktomi

whispered again to him, "You have got her into one of my snare cobweb nets."

But Sandhill Crane again asked Chief Eagle Woman, "It is not true that what you knew were the official reports of the individual members of the committee of which you are the head; therefore, they are facts of the whole affair?"

"Yes," she replied.

The beautiful Swan Chief Woman was then called to tell what she knew. Sandhill Crane was much impressed by the dignity as well as the grace and beauty of the woman, and he carefully surveyed his own chief's regalia, and assumed the air of a gentleman; with his clear and resonant voice, he addressed her: "You are chief on arrangement of the work of the mothers, are you not?"

"I am," she replied with dignity and grace.

"Please tell, in your own way, to the honorable Sachems, your work," he asked.

"As I have not the common social acquaintance with many of the mothers, I classified the committee members in a manner so that each one has the overseeing of the group of mothers whom they knew socially. Each of the committee members reported to me of her group, daily. In this way, I knew definitely what took place in their work every day," she told him.

"Are these women, I mean the mothers, selected because of their virtue and high character and honesty?"

"It is so," she replied.

"Then you have implicit faith in them, and their word is given as vows?"

"Yes, that is true."

"Has there been harmony and peace among them?"

"It was so, until lately."

"How did you know that?"

"By their word of mouth, and actions, and their official reports to me."

"What, for instance, was the trouble between the bird mothers and the insect mothers? To the best of your understanding, officially, do you know that cause of the trouble?"

"By the official reports, Unktomi, they say, was the trouble-maker."

"Did you do anything to stop these troubles?"

"Yes."

"Did you succeed?"

"No."

"Why?"

"It has become tribal and racial bad blood," she replied.

Bumblebee: "Good Woman Swan, is Unktomi one of the mothers in disguise?"

Before the woman answered the question, there was a laugh, in which Unktomi joined.

"No," she replied.

"Is Unktomi a member of your committee?"

"No," she answered.

"Do you know Unktomi personally?"

"I have seen him," she replied.

"Where and when—please tell us."

"I have seen him go by many different times."

"Did you ever talk with him in reference to your work?"

She replied, "No."

"Why not?"

"Because I do not like him—he is unclean and tricky."

"Did he ever play any trick on you?"

"No," she replied.

"Then how do you know he is tricky?"

"I heard so."

"Is it a rumor?"

"Yes."

"That's all. Wait a moment, good woman, one more question. Are you prejudiced against him on account of rumors?"

"Yes," she replied.

Then it was that the pretty young mother, Humming Bird, was called.

Sandhill Crane: "Where were you born?"

Humming Bird: "On a branch of a cedar, over a rosebud slope, on the sunside butte," she replied.

"When?"

"In early summer."

"Were you one of the selected mothers who mothered the man-child?"

"Yes."

"What particular duties, if any, were you assigned to do?"

"The smoothing and softening of the inside of the child's cradle."

"Anything else?"

"On the watch when he sleeps."

"In the night time, or during the day?"

"During the day."

"Were you on the watch while the other mothers nursed and took care of him?"

"Yes."

"Was there anyone else who had the same duties besides you?"

"Yes."

"Who was she?"

"The Oriole Mother and the Chickadee in the day time, and little Owl Mother and Cricket in the night."

"Who is the best mother under your observation?"

"The Robin mother."

"Who is the next?"

"The Swallow mother," she replied.

"Under what mother does the child fret most?"

"All the insect mothers."

"Which ones in particular?"

"Mosquitoes, Ants, and Black Flies," she answered.

"Why do these mothers fail to comfort and quiet the child as do the other mothers?"

"Because they do not soothe it but torment it—they seemed to enjoy his screaming."

"Did you report this truth to your chief women, Eagle and Swan?"

"I did."

"What, if anything, did they do to save the child from annoyance?"

"They called all the mothers together, and before them all, they reprimanded the insect mothers."

"What happened?"

"The insect mothers were very mad, and they charged the Chief Eagle Woman and Swan with discrimination and unfairness to them."

"Then what happened?"

"They said they would tell Unktomi, and if necessary they would complain against us to the Great Eshnaicage."

Bumblebee: "Little woman, did you ever have trouble with the insect mothers in your life?"

"Yes," she replied. "They always visited my home when I was absent, and overrun and tormented my children."

"Then naturally, like all good mothers, you are not friendly with them."

"No, no one else is."

The sweet singer, pretty young mother, the Oriole was called.

Sandhill Crane: "Were you one of the mothers appointed to take care of the motherless child the Great Eshnaicage brought?"

"Yes."

"What were your duties, if any, besides the ordinary duties of mothering the child?"

"I was appointed to supply music for the child's happiness."

"How did you do this work?"

"I and Meadowlark Mother got all the singers of the nation to come and sing for the child."

"What other duties were you assigned?"

"I was also appointed to watch in secret the treatment of the child by different mothers."

"Who appointed you?"

"Chief Swan Woman."

"To whom did you report?"

"To Swan Woman."

"Do you know little Humming Bird Woman?"

"Yes."

"How did you come to know her and when?"

"I have known her for a long time, and then she was one of the secret scout women of the Chief Swan Woman."

The Oriole Woman corroborated all that the Humming Bird had testified. And so all the witnesses of the bird tribes testified to the trouble among the mothers.

Then Unktomi's speaker brought the first witness of the insects; Ant Woman was called. Bumblebee, after asking age and so forth, asked, "What is your occupation?"

"I am a mother of many children, and a tiller and miner's wife."

"Were you one of the mothers of the man-child?"

"Yes."

"Tell the Sachems the experiences you had while engaged in taking care of the child of the Great Eshnaicage."

"Oh, it was not easy work for us the mothers; in the first place, the chiefs of the women council did not give us a fair chance. Secondly, they had secret watchers to watch us. These reported against us to Chief Woman Swan. She disgraced us before all the other women."

"What was the complaint against you?"

"The secret watchers reported that we annoyed and tormented the child to death."

"What did you really do to the child?"

"We found, in the first place, that the child was over-fed. He was in a dangerous state, as a result."

"What would this lead to in the child's life?"

"Why, it would have killed him, or else he would have grown up to be like Eayah. Secondly, he would have never walked, and would have had a hard time to harden his bones or get his teeth. So, we decided to give him medicine; at the same time, all the Ant mothers opened his pores, and the Mosquito mothers performed bloodletting. Of course, the child did not like the medicine—no child ever does. He screamed, but soon after, he laughed and played and was brighter. But the watchers only reported his screams and not the good we did him. Of course, no self-respecting woman would allow herself to be reprimanded without any protest. They would have killed the child in a short time. The Swan and Eagle women took the breast feathers, which were full of vermin that were poisoning him, too. We put medicine on, and ruffled the work of the Humming and Oriole mothers; that was one reason they reported against us. But let me tell you, these bird mothers are forever killing our children to feed their children; yet they sneer at us."

"Did Unktomi tell you to fight against them?"

"We had him with us at one of our councils, but we had already decided to complain to Eshnaicage."

"That is all," said the Bumblebee.

One after another of the little people corroborated the Ant mother's story. The questioning of Sandhill Crane did not change anyone's story. The Sachems had very closely observed, listened to, and noted the testimonies of the witnesses on both sides. Now the defense called the accused, Unktomi himself, who was the keenest of all of them in watching the trial, and knew every discrepancy and flaw in their evidence.

Bumblebee: "Chief Unktomi, where were you born?"

"I don't remember."

"Where did your parents say you were born?"

"They did not say."

"What? Don't you know the country you came from?"

"From the country from which all the creatures came."

"Where do you think that country is?"

"You will have to ask the Great Spirit; no living creature knows. It is the secret of the Great Mystery."

"When were you first conscious of your existence, in what part of the Earth?"

"I was on the warm side of the breast of the Earth."

"Where was that?"

"It was on the sunny side."

"Then where did you go?"

"I went everywhere."

"To what tribe do you belong?"

"To all of them."

"How can that happen?"

"I was adopted either by marriage or relationship by all of them."

"Then you must know something of the customs and habits of all of them."

"I do."

"Do you know any of the mothers who have charge of the man-child?"

"I know them all."

"Do you consider yourself well acquainted with any of them?"

"Yes."

"Did any of them ever talk over matters concerning the man-child with you?"

"Yes, often."

"Did you know Chief Eagle Woman personally?"

"Yes."

"Do you know Chief Swan Woman personally?"

"I do."

"Did you ever discuss the welfare of the man-child with Chief Eagle Woman?"

"I did, many times."

"Did she ever discuss with you, that she was dissatisfied with some of the mothers?"

"Yes."

"What mothers?"

"The insect mothers."

"Do you ever talk these same matters with Chief Mother Swan?"

"Yes."

"Did she tell you the causes and reasons for their dissatisfaction in the work of the insect mothers?"

"Yes."

"Did you tell them your views in the matter or express yourself on either side of the matter?"

"Yes."

"What did you do or say, if anything, on the subject?"

"I praised and encouraged them all in the work they were doing."

"Why, then, do they always suspect you?"

"Because it is their habit, and ignorance."

"Did you ever incite one set of mothers against another?"

"I always urged them to be correct in dealing with one another."

"What is your motive in going among them all as you do?"

"Teaching them to think, that is all."

Chief Sandhill Crane said, "The questions I was to ask Unktomi have been asked by his own speaker—I will ask him only a few."

Sandhill Crane: "Unktomi, did you ever kill anyone?"

"Yes."

"Who was the person?"

"Eayah."

"What was your motive in killing him?"

"Because he was dangerous to us all, and the killing of him will make the rest of the world happier."

"Is it not true, you want to be the great chief of all the people of the whole country?"

"Yes. You ask a foolish question; what else is there on Earth that you strive for? It is the law of the Earth. One good turn deserves a reward."

"That's all," said Sandhill Crane.

Unktomi returned to his speakers. The people were much excited as the speaker, Sandhill Crane, was getting himself ready to present the evidence against Unktomi to the Sachems in a most finished rhetoric, abounding with solipsism and sophistry. It was a graceful oratory, delivered by a graceful and gifted voice of his race. The bird tribes were thrilled and charmed. The speaker himself was graceful and faultlessly attired. When he finished, the voices of the tribes rent the air with cheers.

But when all this was subsided, Unktomi slowly laid aside his raccoon skin robe and walked into the council circle. He was nude and not any too graceful, inclined to lowliness and modesty. The great actor, in his soul, was laughing and elated, because he found himself in a situation he loved the best, and natural.

First, he held both opened hands to Eshnaicage, then to the aged Unktehe; after this most reverent recognition of the high officials, he turned to the Sachems and raised one hand, then dramatically swept the same hand over and toward the audience and the populace, for he knew he was the picturesque hero of the situation, though he was the accused culprit and prisoner before the people of the world and Eshnaicage, the Spirit Messenger. Where could anyone find such a gathering to play for?

"Oh, Great Eshnaicage—oh, Aged Unktehe. Ye, the wise Sachems, and the people of the world! Hear what I have to say in self-defense and in answer to my accusers.

"I am of this Earth; I was born of the fire and the water. A body and a mind were given to me, as you see and know. I lived among the people of the Earth, and I have visited every part of Mother Earth's body, even went to the bottom of the deep water with the Great Sea Turtle to get the Sacred Ritual of Life and knowledge and all its secrets. I did this to teach the people (common) of the world the truth of life on Earth. The Great Medicine Men expelled me from the Sacred Ritual because I teach the truth openly, and they in secret and in pledges. Thus I have demonstrated to the common people the wrongs and rights alongside, so they may better understand. They accused me of trickery. I did not make 'right and wrong,' nor did I invent 'bad and good.' Far less do I introduce 'thinking and reasoning.' He who caused these is alone responsible. Some of you have considered me a tricky politician, because I have tried to show thinking and reasoning by contrast. How can you know bad or wrong if you never saw it? But you have been insistent in practicing deception and wronging without knowing. You bird people are proud, and considered yourselves a superior race, because you were given pretty garments and easy transportation. You have been living on the little people. How can you despise, denounce, and sneer at them, and at the same time eat them?

"There has been given to every creature a weapon of self-defense. Yes, even the grass and the trees have a weapon, a sharp spear, knife, or a poison. Some have their protective weapon in their mind. In this way, I have mine. The mind is my bow; reasoning is my bowstring, and the thoughts are my arrows. Some are crooked; others are straight. I shoot straight arrows and use them for my protection. I come now before you to protect myself against your wrong shooting.

"You have failed in your charges against me. You have only proved your bad spirits against the little mothers, and they resented. I hope the people accept Eshnaicage's good teaching. I am done."

When Unktomi got up to speak, many of the young people laughed at him, but one rap on the council drum from the aged Seer, Unktehe, and all was quiet. As he proceeded they were more and more impressed, until they were wrapped in ominous solemnity. He rose up in eloquence and logical reasoning. They were astounded, and at the end, he swayed them to his way of thinking.

Without any hesitation, the Sachems declared him not guilty. Thus Unktomi won over the animal people again.

My good children, you must not think the bad or trickery won over the good. Unktomi is showing how the bad and the good will always fight throughout physical life.

9

The Training and Rescue
of Little Boy Man

MY DEAR LITTLE FRIENDS: WE HAVE FINISHED THE LEGEND
of Unktomi's trial before Eshnaicage, the Great Medicine Man,
and Unktehe of the animal people. I did not tell you the principles, morals, and customs that came from the trial, because it
was the sacred duty of your parents to explain them in detail by
your home fireside.

These truths come down to us from that far-off time. Their
emotions, propensities, love, and jealousies, we have inherited
from them. They are our traits and customs in a somewhat mod-
ified way. As we proceed with the story of the little man-child,
you will see how it all came about.

As you heard, Unktomi admitted that he was a child of
the Earth and the Sun, just like all creatures of the Earth; only
he claimed he was more imbued with the things of the Earth,
and the intelligence that goes with it. He was an adventurist,
gambling on the lives and affairs of the animals as they were
developed. Keep in your mind clear, these different epochs and
periods in the progress of life on the Earth.

The mothers, in spite of the difficulties they had among
them, especially between the bird and the insect mothers, succeeded in raising the baby man to a robust little boy man; so he
was called by them, the Little Boy Man. He had their milk and
their food; therefore he inherited some of their body traits, as

well as many of their mind traits, but after all, it was the traits of Mother Earth.

It was also, as it definitely appears, that the enmity of the birds and the insects was established; other events later on made it permanent.

It was the desire of Eshnaicage to further teach the animals to understand the man who was to be their master. In view of the purpose, he told the Little Boy Man to go and live with the animals, first with one tribe and then another, until he has learned all their ways and customs. He did this to prepare him for his part in life on this Earth, so that he may intelligently deal with them, and also his experiences with them will make him a wise ruler.

The Little Boy Man, at first, did not want to leave his loving big brother, Eshnaicage, for he had always called him "my Big Brother." It was not easy for either to part; Eshnaicage was tenderly attached to the boy. In turn, the Little Boy Man loved his Big Brother, who was such a big protection to him. Thus as a child and boy, he had seen all the animals of the world, especially the mothers who nursed and took care of him, and he had played and frolicked with their little children.

But Eshnaicage had taken him back to his teepee, and there he taught and showed him the spiritual mind and soul—whence goodness and happiness come. There are, to be sure, goodness and happiness which come from the Earth and the Sun in all their forces in their dominion, but these are temporary, like occasional sunshine, and their quick brilliant lights mislead the body mind, and often mistake them for the real goodness or happiness.

Therefore, Eshnaicage took pains to show him the difference, and told him to be careful of these matters. He then told him in order to receive and possess goodness and real happiness, he must suffer self-denial of the material, sweet, and pleasure-giving things, and practice moderation. To succeed he must have patience and self-control, which is the balance of his mind; then harmony comes to his real mind and soul. When in such a state of his soul, he is in the presence of the Great Mystery. He must not fear the distress of the body, such as pain, hunger, or thirst, and the pain of the mind, based on material and temporal things. He must regard and respect and allay it, if he but can, with a good will and faith in his spirit. He must be generous in all things. He must help to ease the sufferings of others from these, as well as in himself. For the forces of these things react severely, in time, on those who commit the wrong deed.

He was told this was the compensating law of reward and punishment in the body and mind concerning material things. The Great Spirit is good; little spirits are all good, unless they are too much influenced by the substance of the Earth, which influences the mind. Simply, it is like the light involved in watery atmosphere—a fog. The little self is not bad, but it is blackened or darkened for the time being in the darkness. The body mind called this bad.

The Great Spirit is everywhere at the same time. He hears, sees, and knows everything at all times. So too, the little spirits in the material can go everywhere, and know much when they are freed from the body. Thus, those who are in a deep spiritual faith and attitude can see, hear, and know much, but such a person must be in an unselfish state, and desire no material benefit to himself alone, and it is necessary for all those who are worthy to be benefited. There is some power given to the Earth and the Sun by the Great Spirit, to which their children can appeal, but these we call the lesser spirits. That is why their children can appeal to them when they are in need of the things of the Earth or of the Sun.

("This we call the physical prayer, for war, hunting, or rain," Weyuha put in. "There is much more I can tell you, but you are too young yet. I will wait until you are older and have experience in observation. This is enough for you at this time. You must not consider yourself superior to the animal people; if you do, you will offend their spirits.")

"Remember, if anyone abuses you without cause, call me. I will be there instantly. Go, my little brother, and enjoy a boy's life—freedom!" said the Great Teacher.

Eshnaicage had provided his little brother with certain magic strength and transportation, but had cautioned him not to use it unless it was an absolute necessity. He preferred the boy should develop and practice patience and self-control, to make him brave and manly—a broka, he-man.

"Where and to what tribe shall I go to live with first, Brother?" Little Boy Man asked his brother.

"It is for you to choose," he replied.

"Do you not think I should go to Mother Eagle Woman, who was my Chief Mother, when I was little?" the boy asked.

"You must begin to think for yourself, for that is what you must achieve and hand it down to your offspring."

"Well, then I will go to Mother Eagle Woman," he decided.

So the Little Boy Man went to the Home of Chief Eagle, way up on top of the mountain. They live in the very simplest way of all people, with very rough beds, and eat only once or twice in ten days, but sometimes go without it for a much longer time. Here they have the clearest of air because they lived, much of the time, above all steams and vapors of the rivers and lakes. These conditions made the Eagle children far-sighted and very cool-nerved, which enables them to have self-control and hence, bravery. For these reasons, they get into less trouble and little worry.

It was hard for the Little Boy Man at first; therefore, there was temptation to change and go to some other people who had an easier life. But that would be denying himself the strength he needed in his adventure among the people of the world, and then he would have no example to teach his children along the line of the Eagle's philosophy and achievements. So he tightened his breechclout string closer to his stomach, for it was empty and baggy. In the night, he pulled his knees up close to his chin to keep himself from freezing, as the night in the upper air was not as it is at a campfire.

Chief Eagle took him out with his own sons to hunt. They traveled over a vast country. He showed him how to recognize objects on the surface of the Earth. Then he trained the young boy how to shoot from the sky like a straight arrow, and hit the object perfectly. Then he showed him how to fast on the top of the highest mountain. All this was the severest of training, but the Little Boy Man bravely went through them all.

At last Chief Eagle said to him, "Boy, your bravery and faith have won you a feather." So he gave him an Eagle feather from his tail feathers. "This shall be the measure of honor, bravery, and good deeds among your coming race."

But the Eagle Mother had given him a downy little feather which she stuck on his head. "For," she said, "this will distinguish you from the other men of the people." That was growing there amidst his jet black hair.

("In this way, among our people, the Eagle feather is the badge or medal of honor," Weyuha added.)

The Chief Eagle, having trained the boy, sent him back to Eshnaicage. The Chief Eagle was made the chief of all the bird people, as a reward for his service in training the boy, by Eshnaicage.

After this, Eshnaicage kept him for a while to understand

and master what the Chief Eagle had taught—why they were so. Then it was that Eshnaicage invited the Grizzly War Chief and Medicine man to come to his feast. He said to him, "I want you to train my little brother in the customs of your people and your medicines."

To this the Grizzly replied, "We are people of hard experiences—your brother will not endure them."

"That is why I asked you; he needs such training. Do not spare him. He needs hard experience to make him a worthy father and leader," Eshnaicage said to him.

"My little brother, I love you; I want you to be a brave and good man when you grow up. Therefore, I have asked War Chief and Medicine Man Grizzly to take you to his people and train you. Do not let them know you ever feared. When you are tried to your last strength and you feel you have done your utmost, call me. I will come to save you. But be sure you have done all you could."

With these words and advice, the Little Boy Man went home with the Grizzly War Chief.

He was first put into the Sacred Sweat Bath, to clear him of all other people's influence about him. Then they made him a member of the tribe. He was then brought out to wrestle with one of the powerful young warriors. "Ah! Am I going to wrestle with this Little Boy Man? I shall not be blamed if I squeeze him to death," he remarked.

All the people came to see the contest. All the trees and grounds were occupied by the bear spectators. The boy looked harmless; the grizzly athlete was powerful looking and rough. In the first rush, he threw the boy over his head, amid the war whoops, growls, and grunts of the bears. When he turned around to see where he had thrown the boy, he was surprised to see him standing ready to come at him. The yell for the Little

Boy Man was deafening. The big bear madly rushed for him, but the boy was just like a round granite rock. The bear was neither able to hold or lift him up, for the Little Boy Man slipped away from him at every effort. Now the cheer for the little boy was echoed throughout the forest. The bear desperately struck at him with his powerful paw, to no effect, only breaking his own wrist. He continued bravely with one hand, for no grizzly ever knew when he was defeated. At last, with tongue sticking out and soaked with perspiration, he fell over and died. The Little Boy Man had some magic power. He won.

The Bear people marveled at his wonderful bravery. In the first place, they wondered at his great courage and daring to face such a powerful warrior in a great contest, and secondly, his true modesty. He was admired and honored. In the midst of the ovation, Unktomi appeared.

"Ah, my little younger brother. Surely you have shown these boastful Bear people, the power of intelligence. I have often told them that there would come a time when another race of intelligence would show them that they are not the superior people. Well, my younger brother, let us chum together to discuss these things," he said with a most cordial and familiar manner.

But the Little Boy Man was aware of his ambitions, so he said modestly, "Unktomi, I had luck, but the next time I may not succeed as well. I am just learning and trying to get some experience." He was a great athlete.

It is true that Unktomi, when he saw the wonderful skill displayed by the little boy, had said to the Bear Chief, "It will be wisdom on our part to watch this little boy of Eshnaicage," and he began a propaganda against the little boy from that time on.

It was then that the chief of the great Bear people in council decided that the Little Boy Man had fairly won their confidence and deserved to know all their medicine and secrets. Thus they taught him all their war, healing, and hunting medicines.

When the Little Boy Man had returned from the Bear people, Eshnaicage complimented him, saying, "You have done well; I am satisfied with your progress. You shall next go to the Turtle people," he told his brother.

Unktomi had surmised that the boy's mysterious strength in so delicate a body was the work of Eshnaicage. So he had told the animal people on every opportunity, that there was something mysterious about how the Little Boy Man was brought into their country. "The world is full of people, and there is enough to occupy and worry our minds; there is no necessity of another race to share our troubles. I fear this Little Boy Man may become master of us all." Having those ideas in his mind, he made it his business to appear wherever the boy was in training, and always tried to get something out of him to verify his views, and further, to use in his missions against him.

The Little Boy Man, having been with the Land Turtle people for some time, and having learned and received all their medicines and secrets, went to all the other tribes who had adopted him in succession, and learned all their customs and their medicines of life, except the Great Medicine People of the Deep Water (ocean). Eshnaicage again prepared him for his last and important event.

All this time, Unktomi was busy carrying on his propaganda against the life and progress of the boy. He did his work carefully, under cover and excuses.

The Little Boy Man had reached the lower world, which was negotiated and arranged by his Big Brother, Eshnaicage, and the Great Medicine people had given their consent. But when he arrived there, Unktomi had been down there some time before him. By his eloquence and logic, he had persuaded the Medicine Men, if they were wise and clever they could get out of the boy some of Eshnaicage's secrets, and he told them how to manage it and how to treat the boy. "He loves this little boy; he is his special child. He will do anything to relieve him of any distress. We can explain to him that the boy has broken his pledge and disobeyed the Sacred Ritual, and the result is the punishment of the Sacred Laws. Bind him, and put him in one of your secret caves," he advised. "If you are not wise, and just obey Eshnaicage, this boy will steal all our secrets, and then rule us at his own will. Surely you will not permit such a calamity to befall our people, we who are the first people of the Earth," he argued.

Out of a dark cave, a voice cried, "Oh, my brother. I am now nearly all bones, wrapped in my skin. I have tried to be brave, but I cannot endure it much longer. Oh, help—help—my brother."

A flash of the boy's spirit passed through Eshnaicage's tee-pee, and he heard the voice of his little brother. He followed the trail of the Spirit back to where it came from, in an instant, and saw the boy's situation.

"He! He! Misunka, misunka, tewahinda! (Oh, my poor brother, dear to me). I will be with you, my little brother; cheer up!" he spoke aloud, in spirit to him.

Then he hastily called all the animal chiefs in a council, and asked them where his Little Boy Man was, and if there was any trouble come to him. They all said they did not know of any trouble that had come to him. They claimed they were not party to any wrong to him. He desired them to confess if they had anything to do with the boy's distress.

Having satisfied himself that the animal people of the upper world had nothing to do with his brother's distress, he hastily departed to save him. When he reached the shore of the Big

Water, he found the chief of the Medicine people and his wife were basking themselves in the warm surf of the waves. They had come up from the deep to their favorite resort. Eshnaicage instantly turned himself into a great pine stump. The woman said to her husband, "I never saw that stump there before."

"Ugh," said the Big Water Chief. "That stump has always been there."

Just then, they took a nap, and Eshnaicage stepped up and stabbed their sides with his spear. They struggled to flee, but he stopped them. "You may go home and tell your people, Eshnaicage is displeased with them." The two reptiles disappeared under the waves.

Then it was Eshnaicage started to the deep to rescue his little brother. In succession, he disguised himself as he passed through the different nations of the water country, until he reached the country of the Medicine people. It was as he traveled on one of their trails, he overtook an old Sea Turtle Medicine man. He asked him where he was going. The Medicine man replied, "I am called to the sick bed of the Great Chief of the Medicine people and his wife," he replied.

"Ah, ah, what was the disease?"

"It is dreadful. Eshnaicage had wounded them while they were visiting their sunning place upon the surface of the sea," replied the old man.

"Oh, good Medicine man, let me have your medicine pouch. I am a good Medicine man; perhaps I can be useful to them."

"No one has been able to help the old man and his wife. They have tried all their Medicine men," the old man replied.

With the old man's garb and his medicine pouch, Eshnaicage was admitted into the sick chief's teepee. As he entered the teepee, he saw a garment of his brother's. He said under his breath, "My poor little brother."

The teepee was full of their Medicine men, and Unktomi was among them. "Oh, he said, 'my poor little brother.' He must be Eshnaicage," remarked Unktomi to the man next to him.

"Ah, he would not come so far; you are mistaken," the other replied.

When Eshnaicage sat down, the leader of the Medicine Men there said, "Brother Sea Turtle, you may try your medicine. We have all failed."

In reply, Eshnaicage said, "I wish you all would leave me alone with them; perhaps then my medicine would act."

When all the Medicine Men had left, he told the two sick people who he was. "You are guilty of punishing my little brother, without his doing any wrong, and further, you plotted against him. You shall die, and your kind will never live on this Earth again. Your tribe is condemned." He gave each a medicine and soon both were dead.

Eshnaicage then visited his little brother. He was nothing but a skeleton. He took him in his arms and departed for the upper world, where he put him in a sacred sweat lodge and soon got him well.

10

The War of the Animals against Waceheska

MY GOOD CHILDREN, YOU HAVE HEARD HOW THE
Little Boy Man was made to suffer because Unktomi induced
the Great Medicine People of the Big Water to force him to
tell them some of the medicine and the secrets of life, which
they suspected Eshnaicage was teaching him. They were made
to believe by Unktomi's arguments that the boy was brought
forth by his Big Brother on the Earth to rule them. He will be
destructive to the animal people. These Great Medicine people had been gathering wisdom for their race, therefore were
very wise as far as earthly knowledge is concerned. But they
fall to the same mistake that all creatures did, up to that time,
and always will; that is, they put the material things above the
spiritual. They had been given to know how the material things
came about to form a body, by the seeds in the little air cells,
water in the bubbles, and the earth-pebbles, stirred by the heat
of the Sun. They may see all these in action, if they have good
eyes, with the aid of the water and the Sun's reflections; they
may even measure it. But they did not realize that they were
not allowed to find out and measure the spirit, the real power,
or essence of life. It is a lasting secret, until one becomes a good
spirit, and without a body (material).

While these Medicine Men knew so much of the Earth
things, they were autocratic, and they thought they were entitled to know even the secrets of the Great Mystery. This will
always be so, and such people will destroy themselves in the

end. They become destructive of Nature, and since they are part of that Nature, they destroy themselves.

Remember, this was when the animals were the only people on the Earth. The knowledge of the earthly things is good for our bodily well-being, but without the spirit influence, it is dangerous to the possessor of it, and to those who are his neighbors. This intelligence continued from animal to the man, as I call your attention to it now, that you may understand it better in the study of the man.

When Eshnaicage received his little brother, the boy was much disheartened because of his experiences. Apparently the Little Boy Man felt, what will happen to him if his brother was not there to help him? He had, by this time, found out the character of the animal people and Unktomi among them, to advise and scheme. Although he had not complained of his situation on the Earth, with so many scheming and jealous people, he felt the outlook for him was not so promising. Yet he had in him the true principles, which had taken root in his soul, by the association and companionship of his Big Brother. So he was not willing to have him know his unhappy thoughts.

Of course, Eshnaicage was aware of this, and prepared to teach and strengthen him further. In view of these thoughts, the kind and loving brother kept him within his observation until he grew into handsome, noble young manhood. He was shown the nature of goodness, truth, and virtues. The roots and trunk of true life were plainly explained to him. Then he was told what the leaves, flowers, and seeds of such a life will be. He had personally observed and experienced, therefore knew, what physical life with its intelligence is. The animals and the elements, with all their attendant forces and burdens, he had seen.

For a long time, Eshnaicage was teaching the elemental and fundamental principles of life, and the cause and effect. When he was well trained and had been taught all these things, the Big Brother said:

"My brother, you are grown up, so you must go among all the animals and let them understand you. They must now understand that you are in body conformed to this Earth's own laws, but you have a spirit conscious of the Great Spirit. Their spirit, although sprung from the same source, is only conscious of the spirits of the Earth and the Sun; therefore, they are always conscious of what is going on within the influence of these two. They are the Medicine men of that sphere.

"You must respect their rights, when not opposing to your spirit. You must love them all; your body is as frail as theirs, and some of them have more strength and convenience in traveling than you have. Be careful of their rights and wishes, for many of them have good minds and virtues, also are kind-hearted. Be patient and fair with them. In this way they will trust and serve you," he advised.

The Little Boy Man was now not only a handsome young man, but gentle and noble. He had a downy white feather growing upon his head, which was very good to look at.

When he entered the country of the Bear people, he was well received and welcomed, because they had not seen him for a long time. "Oh, oh! He has a white feather on his head! He is a chief. We will call him 'White Feather on His Head' (Waceheska)." So in this way he got his name thereafter, among all the animals. No longer was he called "Little Boy Man."

For many winters he lived, studied, and traveled among them, to further establish the relationship between man and the animal people. Because he was so handsome and noble, many of the young women of the different tribes made love to him, but he did not know what that meant. He just loved them all alike, same as sisters to him.

All the while, Unktomi was busy studying him and making comments on his peculiarities, and never overlooked any opportunity to impress them that, under cover of innocence, he was stealing all their secrets and medicines, to become their ruler and chief. He cautioned them to be careful and watch him.

Finally, again Unktomi's propaganda took hold in their minds. He had said, cunningly, "Make manly war on him, by all the animals of the Earth!"

"But," some of them said, "he has not done us any harm."

"Ugh, we can fix that up; we can say he has broken the laws of the Sacred Ritual. One of the first laws of the Earth is to be married and have children. This young man cruelly insults the young women who are nice to him. That will be reason enough to declare war on him. Eshnaicage cannot blame us for this," he assured them.

In this way, the first World War came to pass. All the chiefs were won over to Unktomi's propaganda, and they called a great secret council to decide upon the manner of beginning the war. It was decided just to declare war against Waceheska for breaking one of the principal laws of the Sacred Ritual.

When the secret council of war was concluded, each war chief was authorized to send messengers to all his tribes to recruit their young men for the war. It was decreed by the war chiefs to make their attacks in turns; then they would know what tribe overthrew him and took him for their prisoner.

While this conspiracy was going on, Waceheska was traveling from the western Big Mountains to the broad prairies of the Mississippi-Missouri valleys. He saw Chief Scout Swallow coming from the East. "Woo! Woo!" He gave a war call of a messenger. The happy, easy-going Waceheska sat down on a hill and waited for him. The messenger tried to go around him, but he stopped him.

"Now, my good brother, sit down, and tell me what this war is all about, and against what people."

The messenger was embarrassed and did not want to speak, but Wacheska said, "Brother, it is best to tell the truth, then there will be no argument. I can easily guess what is your message. It will be best for you to tell me."

With many pauses and apologies, the Swallow told Wacheska that Unktomi had induced all the chiefs of the world to declare war against him. Every tribe is notified, and he was sent forth to notify the bird people. All that Wacheska said was, "I am so sorry, for I love the people of the world," and dropped his fine head upon his big chest.

"Go on; do what you were told to do," he told the messenger.

When the messenger left him, he filled his pipe to smoke, because he was much depressed. As he smoked, thinking deep thoughts, there appeared at a distance, another messenger of the people, coming from the South. "Woo! Woo!" he too called. When he saw the man on the hill, he paused to see who it was When he finally recognized him, he also tried to go around him, but Wacheska called him.

"Ah! Ah! Brother Buffalo, I know you are going on an important errand, but just sit down and have a whiff of my pipe," he said to him.

When they had finished their smoke, Wacheska silently emptied the ashes from the bowl of his pipe and laid it on the ground. "I know your mission, but that is a matter for the people; I wish you a good journey," he told him.

The young buffalo messenger said, "It is not our people's fault. It is the chiefs' fault, who listened to Unktomi," he apologized and explained.

After this, Wacheska was still sitting on the hill thinking. Meanwhile, he saw other messengers going in every direction all over the country. He took a long breath and uttered a deep sigh; "I love my people," he said aloud.

When he left the hill to go to his brother's teepee, which was pitched in the middle of the Earth (Sioux supposed it to be at the southwest corner of the state of Minnesota, at the Pipestone Quarry), he was sad and unhappy because he was a peaceful man, and war means destruction of the animals.

When Eshnaicage saw his brother Waceheska was preoccupied and sad, he asked him why he was so downhearted. He replied, "I am unhappy because all the people of the Earth have declared war on me, and I do not understand why they should. I love them all, and I have not done anything to harm them."

"Cheer up, my brother, you have committed no harm against them. You are not, therefore, responsible for any suffering or calamity that the war may bring upon them," Eshnaicage told him.

"But Brother, I do not want to kill any of them. You have taught me to be good. This war means killing. Besides, I am only one and they are many. Furthermore, I have no weapons to fight and defend myself with. Can you persuade them to see the wrong? I am not afraid. Let them kill me, if I have wronged them," the brave young man declared.

"It is true you have committed no wrong; you have not harmed them. But they wish to test your power and my authority. It is well. Let it come—they will learn. I will provide you the means to fight them with, and therefore you must accept their challenge."

So Eshnaicage immediately went about preparing his brother for the World War. He first tossed up into the air a jasper stone, which, when it fell on the ground, made a great jasper wall of great height—nearly a day's travel across it. He did this four times, each time making a wall higher than the preceding one, thus forming a wall within a wall, four deep. He pitched his teepee within it, and went to making bows, bowstrings, arrows, and arrowheads, chipped from the rocks, as well as war clubs of stone, and hatchets and knives.

("The debris of this fort is still to be found on and around the Pipestone Quarry down to Ha-Ha," said the old teacher, Weyuha, referring to Sioux Falls, South Dakota. "My good children, this is where the weapons were made that the first man, the Indian, used," added the teacher.)

While he was thus busy, Unktomi appeared outside the fort, asking for admission. Eshnaicage told Waceheska to let him in. When he came inside, he was astounded to see the new and formidable weapons of war.

"Ah, ah, Great Eshnaicage, it has been a very hard struggle for me to persuade these ignorant and headstrong people from bringing a war upon your brother, as they are very jealous of his intelligence and accomplishments. Indeed, they are afraid he will, some day, become their master. I come to tell you, before they attack, that this has been agitating their minds for a long time. I want to assure you, I have done my best to prevent it, but it was no use." Unktomi was playing the game on both sides, to cover his guilt in fomenting and inciting the animal people to make this war.

("But you must remember, this is the rule of the dishonest propagandist among the people since that far time. They usually think themselves smart, and that their doings will never be discovered. But such wrongdoings are all marked against the Great Spirit's clear sky. Therefore, when the sun shines, it appears and it is known," commented Weyuha.)

The wily scout, Unktomi, was deceiving himself, and he left, satisfied in his own mind; he thought he had done well for himself by hoodwinking Eshnaicage and Waceheska. But it was not true, for they knew his part, although it was not time to expose him, for the world must have this lesson.

The day was calm, and there was a clear blue sky above. Eshnaicage had advised his brother to arrange all his weapons on the flat tops of the walls conveniently for his use. He was still engaged in this work, when he saw on the horizon that the black masses of the animal warriors were coming. As they approached, their war cry was terrible. It was the first time the peaceful spirit of Waceheska had been aroused. He was thrilled through and through, and found himself answering with threatening war whoops.

Each nation was attacking him from different angles. Masses of the big animals hurled themselves against the massive walls of the fort without any effect, while the diggers were busy boring holes underground. But Eshnaicage was a great builder; he had made the fort twenty paces deep underground.

At first, Waceheska paid little attention to these. He was fighting the animals who attacked by air. Whenever he shot an arrow, there was truly a rain of stone-headed arrows. Each time he brought down millions of the bird people. Thousands of the climbers and creepers reached the top of his first defense. These he knocked off by one stroke of his stone war club. He fought a long time, when he was forced to the last defense, high up. He appealed to his brother.

"Oh, Brother! New sets of warriors have come, and they are overpowering me, for they are into my eyes, nose, and ears and all over me! What shall I do?" he shouted. It was the insect nations. Then it was that Eshnaicage answered him from his tee-pee, "Strike your war club on the walls of the fort."

"Woo! Woo," he uttered, and struck the wall with his stone tomahawk.

Behold, sparks of fire darted in every direction and the

country took on a prairie and forest fire. The little warriors were swept away in the great flames. This also compelled the large animals to flee to save themselves. But he had already killed millions by his magic arrows. The Earth was full of dead bodies of the creatures.

The wailing of the people for their lost could be heard far, far away, and it even echoed in the sky.

During the interval, all the war chiefs held a council. It was decided to give the water peoples (fishes, etc.) their turn in trying to subdue Wacaheska. They replied that their land allies would have to build dams on the rivers of the country, especially the Mississippi and Missouri, so that their warriors could attack Wacaheska's fort. To this the land animals agreed. Behold, all the streams were dammed, and the waters were menacingly advancing toward the fort.

As soon as the water began spreading over the land, all the land animals took their places upon the mountains to watch the water warriors fight their foe. Then it was that the land between the Western and Eastern Mountains was flooded, and when it reached halfway up to the walls of the fort, the water warriors began to appear upon what had been a vast prairie but was now a big water.

Anticipating all this, Eshnaicage had made some big spears, stone war clubs, as well as big arrowheads, because there were many warriors among the water people. By the time the water went over the first wall, the warriors began to attack the fort. Wacaheska bravely resisted them, for he speared and clubbed many of them. But thousands of half water and full water animals built many dams, which forced the water up higher and higher, until they had the first defenses of the fort under water.

The great monsters of the Big Water now reached the fort. Wacaheska began to lose his courage. "Oh, Brother, they have broken into my defense; I cannot stop the progress of the water," he declared.

"Appeal to the element warriors; they will hear and help you," Eshnaicage advised.

He obeyed; he prayed earnestly to the Element War Chief. In answer, a little fleecy cloud appeared amid the sky. Out of it a little fiery arrow darted like the tongue of a snake. As soon as this was seen, all the Big Sea Monsters gave warning for danger, and forthwith in haste started for the Big Water. But the element warriors were already upon them. Their guns were deafening and deadly to the water warriors. The water was soon full of their dead bodies. The sky warriors (Lightning and Thunder) chased the warriors to the sea. To this day, we still find their bones, which became rocks (petrified) all over the country.

In chasing these water warriors, the sky warriors tore the earth and rocks, also the dam that the animals had made. In this way, all the waters were freed and returned to the Big Water, save those naturally belonging there.

This ends the World War.

My good children, we shall next take up the World Peace following the war, and Waceheska's marriages.

11

The World Peace
and Waceheska's Marriages

MY GOOD CHILDREN, WE HAVE LEARNED IN OUR LAST LESSON
how Unktomi caused the war between all the creatures of the
Earth and the man, Waceheska. In this war, by the help of the
elements, the man conquered them all. We will now take up
what followed.

In the war, the animals were almost destroyed by water and
fire with the wind; only a few of each tribe were left. These were
the more peaceful ones. Before going into this, let me tell you
a few of the customs started from this event, and the legends
which came out of it.

I have told you Eshnaicage made weapons for his brother
Waccheska to use in defending himself against the attacks of the
enemies, the animals. These stone weapons, millions of them of
all sizes, are still to be found all over the Earth. In our legends
we called them Eshnaicage's stone arrowheads, tomahawks, and
spears. Some of the less informed Indians called them Unktomi's
arrows, etc., but this is not true. White people say the Indians made them, but that is not true either, for the simple rea
son that they are not practical; we made many weapons which
were practical and easily made. No Indian will try to make an
arrowhead which will take much time and hard labor, and likely
as not spoil it before finishing; then it proved to be not practical. We only use a four-and-a-half- to five-foot bow and must
carry a very light arrow, only two and a half feet long, and very

straight. Many have no heads, are just sharp, as you know. For hunting birds of all kinds and small animals, we used no arrowheads fixed onto them. We do not know who made them, save the Legend says Eshnaicage made them and that they were shot with supernatural powers. But that is enough for that.

The World Peace, which followed the World War between the animals and the man, was again held at Waceheska's fort at the Pipestone Quarry. Here Eshnaicage made a special stone, out of which a peace pipe was made to be used in the peace council. Thus he made the peace pipe of the Indian world.

It was there and then he laid down the custom that no blood will ever be spilt on that sacred and consecrated peace ground. So from that far-off time to this, no Indians ever fight on that place, although many different Indians from all parts of the country come there to get the rocks for their peace pipes. As far as the Indians know, there is no red pipestone to be found anywhere but this one place. The thickest is only two inches, and it is laid deep under jasper stones. From this place, pipestone is taken to all parts of the Indians' great country (North America).

When the elements helped Waceheska and conquered the animals, they had carried the war into the Big Water, and there killed many of the warlike people, save those who succeeded in reaching their forts (caves) in the far down Big Waters. Then for a long time there was no war. The land between the Western and the Eastern Mountains was depopulated. When the water had gone back to the Big Water, the grass and trees came back and grew again; then what was left of the land animals began to come back to the open country. Meanwhile, Eshnaicage had put Waceheska through a new training. He first put him in a sweat lodge, then made him fast before the Sun and the Earth. He thus prepared him to conform to the body he desired him to establish on the Earth. It took him a long while to do this, but it was accomplished.

One bright day, while Waceheska was standing upon the flat top of his old fort, he saw someone was approaching his fort. He soon discovered it was Chief Mastincatonka (Jack Rabbit). He held forth a big peace pipe with a long stem; the stem of the pipe was embossed with Porcupine's quills, and decorated with Loon's and Drake's neck feathers and scarlet colors of other birds; also two Eagle plumes, and a Buffalo tail suspended from it. The pipe itself was a beautiful shell. This he held in prayer to Eshnaicage and Waceheska, asking for admission.

"How, how, Kola Mastinca! (Welcome, welcome, friend Jack Rabbit!) Enter our teepee," shouted Waceheska. "We are glad you come; what is your message?"

"Oh, great Eshnaicage and brave Waceheska, I come from a great council of the chiefs of the many nations. The women of these nations have declared to the men, they will not allow them to go to war again. They urged their men to make peace with you. The chiefs of the council have appointed me a messenger of peace, because I was the only chief who lifted his voice against Unktomi and the war, which has swept them off the Earth by your bravery." He appealed to both Eshnaicage and Waceheska. He was dressed in a spotless white garment, and no paint on his face. Upon his head he wore two Eagle feathers. It is true, that Chief Mastincatonka has been a peace man. He never carries any weapon. He was, on this account, appointed peace messenger.

Eshnaicage took no part in this peace treaty; he let his man-brother take charge, because it is his affair; he established these customs for his coming human race. The messenger was sent back with the news that Waceheska was willing and glad to meet the leading chiefs and the warriors of all the nations at his fort.

When the appointed time came, all the great chiefs and leaders of the people of the Earth gathered at the Pipestone Quarry.

All that Eshnaicage had to do in this great peace council between the man, Waccheska, and the animal peoples, was to make a peace pipe of the red stone and substitute it for the shell pipe which Chief Mastincatonka had brought, but he retained the stem and its ornaments. This was the Indians' sacred peace pipe, which is now known all over the world.

("The ignorant white people called every Indian pipe a peace pipe," explained Weyuha.)

The country around the Pipestone Quarry was full of people. Eshnaicage only appeared once; that was when he presented the peace pipe. The great chiefs sat in a great circle, and at the north side, Wacheska occupied a place. Everything having been arranged, the peace pipe was passed around. The great Medicine man, the Grizzly Bear, was the first to address Wacheska. "Oh, Great Chief!" he said, "We have come to smoke the pipe of peace. In doing so, we acknowledge your leadership of the Earth. Henceforth we will not listen to Unktomi." As he mentioned his name, Unktomi protested by saying, "This is a peace meeting and hence, there should be no charges against anyone, for that will disturb the peace," although he was only a spectator.

"It is our resolution and desire forever, that there shall be no more general war or uprising against your leadership, oh Chief," said Grizzly Bear. Then he turned about to the assembled chiefs and said, "Hear ye all! You have asked me to say to the Great Chief, Wacheska, that if he agrees not to bring among us a calamity or a devastating war, we pledge ourselves to serve him as long as our Mother Earth has us for her children. He may use, as he needs, every part of our bodies for his food and his comfort. In return for this, and in order to make the treaty binding, he must respect our spirits; he must not destroy our bodies wantonly; he must not abuse and desecrate our bodies. Lastly, and to make this covenant strong, he must intermarry into all our tribes; in this way we will have each other's blood."

When he got through, all the chiefs voiced, "How, how, how!!!" in approval. It seemed unanimous, but it was not. The Great War Chief of the Mosquito nation stepped into the council. Everyone was excited and in suspense, for they did not know what he was about to say.

"Ah, what is this brave and manly act of the people of the Earth? Are you going to blame Unktomi again for this senseless, cowardly surrender of your birthrights? Are you not the boastful nations of yesterday? Ah, ah! The proud first people of the Earth beg to be servants of this newcomer? Let me say, not for us, the insect nations, the first of all the first people of the Earth. Who is he? The Earth is our mother; the Sun is our father; here is our home. This stranger came from somewhere, we know not where."

At this instant Unktomi shouted, "Hear, hear!" among the spectators.

"We, the insect nations, declare to you, we disapprove of this shameful surrender. Are we not entitled to something in this country of ours? This day, we declare this man Wacheska is our enemy. We shall carry on war against him and his children as long as our mother is able to give us strength. We shall bring, each year, warriors, so many that no one can count. We will make him afraid to go away from his very home. We will attack there, too. You boastfully talk about your bravery; we are the only brave people in this world."

As he concluded, many chiefs, especially among the bird nation, declared they would have no mercy on them. So it has been since; the insect people are friends of nobody.

But the treaty was made and was satisfactory to both sides, except that the insect nations did not accept the treaty. Peace was then observed between the man and the animal people, and there was no war, only rivalry in athletic sports among them, also duels, but these were individual affairs. The injuries from these were considered honorable wounds.

The Earth was beautiful, and the nations became large again, and there was plenty of food, so they lived peacefully.

Eshnaicage, as I told you, before this war had trained and showed many new things to his brother. He had prepared him gradually to understand family life and mate love; different from the law he had before this. When the treaty was made, Waceheska was in his agreement with them. He did not fully realize what that meant, until Eshnaicage explained it to him.

"Now," said the Big Brother, "you must travel among them. You will find some of the beautiful maids of the different nations will attract you. It will be powerful and a great happiness to you."

Waceheska had thought the matter over many times, and had not felt the force of it. One beautiful spring, when all the trees and plants were blooming, and the brooks were singing down the mountainsides, and the lakes were blue like the sky, and sparkling—when all the animal people were apparently very happy—everybody put on their new and best garment. He felt the spirit of it, so he too painted his face and adjusted all his garments and his Eagle feathers on his head.

He said to his brother, "I feel like these people; I want to travel for a while." So he went away. He traveled until he was tired and hungry. He camped by a beautiful mountain brook. He was absorbed in the beautiful scenery when he heard a lovely liquid voice singing a love song, on the mountainside. He felt strangely moved. Yet as he listened, the song stopped. In a little while, a lovely young woman dressed in dark grey with black trimmings, with a dull red shirt waist, approached him, carrying a basket of cherries. She sweetly smiled at him, saying, "Excuse me, I thought there was no one here." Waceheska was overcome with a strange feeling of happiness, and was strangely drawn toward the young woman. He was so overcome that he did not know what to answer. With much effort, he finally said, "Oh, oh, but it was such a sweet song I just now heard when you came."

"Was it?" she smilingly answered. "Won't you have some berries?"

"I thank you, young woman. Will you not tell me who was the singer?"

"It was, I—I, who just now sang."

"Ah, I love the singer," he said, smiling.

"Yes, but I was singing to my lover, who is to meet me here; we are to be married this evening, and I am out selecting our home," she replied.

"Oh," said the handsome young man. He was so disappointed; he had never had such an experience and feeling in all his life. He felt very badly; he was almost sick, and so discontented he could not bear to stay there. He put on his moccasins and started off again. He came to a lovely lake surrounded by deep woods. Here he built his pine bough teepee for the night. The sun was over the western hills; the hillside above him was full of roses, amidst which there stood a tall dead tree. From a high branch there came one of the sweetest songs that was ever sung in the world. It came, he discovered, from a maiden dressed in brown with a speckled shirt waist. It was so beautiful and sweet that even the old oak trees on the opposite hill bowed their heads to the singer. When the song was finished, she came down to his teepee. She brought some strawberries because, "I know you are a stranger," she said politely.

"Yes, I am a stranger and alone. Are you the young woman who sang so sweetly?" he asked.

"Yes," she answered.

"I would love to have you for my wife," he said bluntly.

"Ah, but you are too late; I am already a wife. My husband is very handsome, and he is a very sweet singer, too."

He stayed there, but he was very restless, as the lake was just full of happy people, singing and laughing and love making, way into the night. As he was sitting by his fire during the moonlit night, he saw in the shimmering pool of water a pretty, shy maiden, industriously carrying an armful of wood. She was dressed in dark brown, and when she got home she fixed the tee-pee. She was busy as she could be. He watched her, and finally he said, "I would like to have a wife like you." She looked up at him, then indignantly slapped the water and ran into the teepee. He saw that night a handsome young man, courting a beautiful, slender, willowy girl, both dressed in brown, reddish garments with white front, and they had slender, lovely limbs and neck. In the early morning he heard a musical laughter in the woods near him; when he looked, he saw the graceful leaps of two young lovers, running from branch to branch, and again suspending themselves on two adjacent swaying limbs. Everywhere he looked there is a joyous love making. He was disappointed in his love impulses and emotions. He was sitting on a rock, under a shade tree, in deep thought. There came Unktomi.

"Ah, my handsome friend, Waceheska, I am so glad to see you. I have been thinking about you since the treaty you made with all these tribes. By the way, in that peace treaty you promised to intermarry. Have you made any arrangements yet? I tell you," he went on, "you want to be very careful, or they are liable to turn over on you some of their old hags. Let me caution you; these people are very tricky, and given to play tricks on some innocent person. Oh, I know them. I have lived with them all my life," he declared. "They have played that trick on me," he added. "Let me be your scout and informer on your love affairs," he suggested. "You know you cannot make love to any of their young women until you adopt their ways and have a body like theirs. Even then you will have some trouble, because their young men are very jealous. I tell you, my good friend, you will have duels every day."

Unktomi, my children, is a philosopher and logician; in his schemes he uses truths and human weaknesses. Because of this system, he wins over people against their will. What he said was historically true, and he knew, in dealing with Waceheska, he had to support his assertions with facts. But he has his schemes in everything he is concerned or interested in. Unktomi is trying to gain the confidence of the animal people by associating himself with Waceheska. But Waceheska had his own medicine in his love affairs, and when the time came for him to use it, he must understand them.

In his first effort on body love (mate love), Waceheska found out he must subject himself to the physical emotions and propensities, as well as their peculiar class of feelings to each other. So he gradually became transformed and accustomed to Nature's way. At last Waceheska understood the ways of body love, and their management. He had, after a long time of traveling, come back to Eshnaicage, and told him of his difficulties; that he felt the force of love and desire, but that the animal people did not seem to understand him. As Unktomi said, he must be one of them in every way. Then it was that Eshnaicage gave him the medicine in love making. The effect was equally troublesome. Every tribe he met, all the young women sought to marry him, and he did marry one of them, but his troubles did not end. The young women sought after him so much that he became annoyed and left the tribe each time. This was heartbreaking for him because he loved his children. In this way, he married among all the different nations.

It was a long time, in this continent, that the land was peo-.pled by the children of Waceheska. These people mixed in every shape and manner among all the tribes. Some of them were very big or very small; some of them very intelligent; some of them very good like the father; some of them very bad; and they all had the same language all over the world.

Eshnaicage had been watching all these people and their habits. There was much complaint to him from all the animal people, against the half man or part animal people. There was much breaking of both the Sacred Ritual and Eshnaicage's new teachings—goodness, virtue, and peace. To be sure, there were some real men people grown up among them, who were handsome and good. But they were all ruled by the bad people and by the same customs.

Now, good children, this is a very confusing part of the Legend, therefore you be careful in the weeding of the bad from the real things. Truth and happy philosophy came out of it. There are many, many legends of Waceheska's love affairs, but these are taught apart from the main Legend.

We shall take up next, what happened to the marriage of Waceheska, and the final establishment of the man as we are, and the end of the creation of the man.

12

The Great Snow and the Departure
of Eshnaicage and Waceheska

MY GOOD CHILDREN, WE WILL NOW TAKE UP THE LAST
period of Eshnaicage's work, in the training and perfecting the
man he made, and his offspring.

The children of Waceheska have not improved the conditions of the all-animal people of the Earth. They have brought
about a new race, who were half man and half animal; their
bodies were neither man nor animal. Indeed, there sprang up a
race of ill-shaped people, except a few who were like Waceheska
in every way; likewise, a few born like their animal mothers.
Their minds, too, were neither man nor purely animal. They
were healthy and intelligent, but reckless and much like the type
of Unktomi. This surprised both Eshnaicage and Waceheska.
It was necessary for Eshnaicage to do something serious with
them. As they had the same language and customs, they were
a race of its own, and the unprincipled class ruled the few good
ones with the rest of the people. This condition demoralized
the people of the Earth. The good ones had a very hard time to
follow the teachings of the Great Teacher.

When Eshnaicage saw the effect of the mixing of the man
and the animal blood, he decided to readjust the state of their
condition. It was a very serious situation, and he felt he must
use severe measures to bring about a new and higher order of
society for Waceheska's children.

He had secretly sent forth his man to advise the best

human-shaped and good ones of his children, both males and females, to isolate themselves from the people by going to the high mountains and diligently building warm houses for themselves, and storing up much food. As these were only a few, scattered all over the Earth, they easily carried out Waceheska's orders, unnoticed by the bad people. This was done without being openly told. Then Waceheska hunted and prepared to raise much corn and tobacco, and stored them in great quantities for himself and Eshnaicage, and also made warm clothing and stored up great quantities of fuel, and built a warm and large teepee.

When all this had been fully accomplished, they moved into their new home. One evening, Waceheska saw big flakes of snow coming down, so he told Eshnaicage. He replied, "I am sorry, but it has to be done." The snowstorm lasted many, many moons, followed by intense cold weather. No one was able to get out to hunt, or to go to their provision caches. The world was completely covered with snow. All the people were starved to death, except the few who were warned beforehand, who had isolated themselves from the crowded villages and camps.

During this storm, Unktomi had again found out what was about to befall the people of the Earth, and he went to work to lay up much food. But, in time, he found himself in want. He had been living on a few roots, but when this was gone he went to call on the people who usually have plenty of provisions. Alas, he found they also had exhausted their supply. He wanted to ask the loan of enough food to last him until the storm was over. He did not know that Eshnaicage had caused the storm to destroy all the undesirable people.

Unktomi, having failed in his purpose, sat down in a cave on the mountainside and began to realize the seriousness of the situation. He said to himself, "Persistency catches the game; I shall try once more. I will go to the most industrious people, the Beaver, the Mice, the Squirrel, the Mole, the Muskrat, the Bees, and the Ants." But they all refused him, saying, "We are a big family, and our supply is getting very low, and we don't know how long this blizzard will last. It would not be right for us to give you the food our children need."

The outlook was not encouraging for him. He finally decided to induce Mastincala, Rabbit, to allow him to live with him for the winter. He knew this person was peaceful and generous and always has plenty of provisions for the winter. Also, he is the greatest hunter in the winter, because he has fine snowshoes. And furthermore, he is the forest man in the winter, when all the people are handicapped by the cold and the snow, and has warm clothes and moccasins. All these facts Unktomi had carefully considered in his own helplessness.

"How, how, Unktomi, come in! I am glad to see you, for I have scarcely seen anyone for some moons."

"Yes, yes, Misun (dear Brother), I thought of you these many days. As you say, there is scarcely anyone able to go anywhere on account of the great storm. I knew you would be lonely; so I have come. I tell you, Brother Mastincala, I have traveled a good ways, and I am very hungry," he told his host. He had only walked a short distance, but he had not eaten any food for several days.

Mastincala replied, "Unktomi, it is too bad, but I myself have to go without it some days, so as to make my provisions last as long as possible. I have only a few roseberries and a small pile of cottonwood barks. You will have to wait until the evening when I can prepare our last meal, then, go to bed."

"It is the best place to go when your stomach is empty," Unktomi replied with a show of thankfulness.

As the two were preparing the simple food, there staggered in Chief Sungila, Fox. He was poor and weak. "Have you anything to eat, Brother Mastincala?" he faintly asked. "I am starving."

"Ah, Brother Sungila, you are just in time; we have just finished the cooking of our meal."

"Oh, I am so hungry," he said.

"Brother Sungila, you are in luck; sit down. Perhaps the smell of the food will make you sick," said the host.

"Yes, yes, you must not eat too much, for it will make you sick," said Unktomi.

"Unktomi, have you any tobacco? Perhaps that will soothe my nerves," Sungila asked, while licking his lips.

"Yes, Brother. I have here just a bowl full. Let us have the pipe of peace, for we will soon not have to smoke," replied Unktomi, humorously, because the food was all they had left.

The three sat by the campfire and discussed the great calamity of the people of the world. "I have said that this Spirit Eshnaicage is not here for fun. He is up to some game; that is a sure thing in my mind. I suspect he is the whole of our trouble. Why, we were very happy upon our mother's lap, the Earth. Why, our parents, the Earth and the Sun, have never punished us, because we are their children. But behold, here comes this Spirit Eshnaicage. He was not satisfied with our ways, we, the Earth Children. He goes and creates a man-child. We have been asked to raise and be good to him. We did as we were told. He grew up and married everywhere, among all the tribes. He brought forth many children. They are worse than the children of the Earth-Sun. They are boastful and think themselves superior, because they can do some things different from us. Now, he is not satisfied with his own children. I tell you, Brother Mastincala and Sungila, he is trying to make us over again. Who is going to be responsible for all our suffering?" he went on, with much dignity and self-satisfaction.

The three went to sleep, hoping something would turn up to save them from starvation.

"Get up, Brothers, Father Sun is in the sky. We shall be saved," shouted Sungila, with much joy, as if someone had brought them some food.

"Ugh," replied Unktomi, "he will have to do some hard snow shoveling to save us from starvation and drowning."

"Cheer up, Brother Unktomi. You are always complaining. The Great Spirit knows his business. All these things are meant for something good and great. When you make your arrows, you spoil many before you make a good one, don't you?"

When they all sat by the campfire, while Mastincala started to put on his snowshoes to go hunting, Unktomi realized that something must be done to save them from starvation. He suggested that the three must go in search of Waceheska's teepee. Surely he must have some food, for he is living with Eshnaicage, and therefore they have food to eat. Just then, Mastincala returned with a few roseberries for breakfast.

Just as the food was divided among them, there came a rough, hoarse voice from outside the teepee. "Whoever you are, enter my teepee," cried Mastincala. The door-flap was lifted, and entered Chief Raven, emaciated and very weak, but yet quite brave. "Ah, Brother Raven, you never have shot a straighter arrow than this, for you have hit a meal. If you had missed it, it would have been the worst one you ever have shot, for you would never have another chance," chuckled Unktomi.

When the scanty meal was finished and they had smoked, Mastincala said, "There is no more food."

"My good Mastincala, the Sun has again smiled on our faces, but I think there is still much danger before us. For when the snow melts, the country will be a big lake. If it is possible for us to find Eshnaicage and Waceheska, it will be wisdom on our part to find out if there is any chance for us to secure a canoe, and some supply of food. Waceheska is so good hearted and generous, perhaps he will ask Eshnaicage to favor us in this our hard situation," said Unktomi.

Mastincala having provided them all with snowshoes, of which he always had plenty on hand, they crawled out of the host's teepee. The Sun was bright and warm, which almost blinded them, because they had not seen it for a long time, having been confined in the snow-cave for many moons.

When they got up in the open they beheld the world was a snow prairie—not a thing to see. The sparkling snow-blanket meets the blue sky at the horizon.

Thus Mastincala, Sungila, Kangi (Raven), and Unktomi started out to look for Eshnaicage and Waceheska's teepee. They had traveled a long ways and had not seen any living thing, when they saw far away, at a distance, a little black speck against the vast prairie of snow. They slowly traveled toward it.

"How, Brothers!" called Unktomi. The others looked back. Unktomi had tripped himself with the tail of his snowshoes, and was so weak that he could not get up.

So, they said, we all have to die, one after another in this manner. "Unktomi, we will have to leave you here."

"Oh, Brothers, there is no greater heroism than helping a fellow brother in misfortune like mine. Draw me in my blanket. Besides, this heroic act will touch the heart of Eshnaicage. He will help us. Don't you see? I am playing this to help you." He cleverly argued them into helping him. Finally, they did as he told them. They dragged him in his own Raccoon blanket, which they made into a toboggan.

When they approached the black speck, they found it to be a cliffside of a high mountain. They soon discovered the smoke came from below it. It was the teepee of Eshnaicage and

Waceheska. A cave on the edge of this cliff was the teepee of the Golden Eagle. Remember, my children, the Eagle and his wife were the first adopted parents of Waceheska, so when this world blizzard came, he had them near him. Besides, he used the Eagle as a scout to look about the country to locate all the mountains to which the selected children of Waceheska and the animals had gone to save themselves. He was also used as a guard for any approach to their teepee. In this way they found out the coming of the party with Unktomi.

At last, they reached the place. Mastincala, the peaceful man, addressed the Great Chief and his brother, "Oh, Eshnaicage, and Father Waceheska, have mercy on us. We have come because we are about to starve." Thereupon, Waceheska came out and led them inside the teepee.

Eshnaicage and Waceheska lived in a beautiful big teepee with many parts, in fact, many teepees within a teepee. It was made of marble stones and ice stones, all the same to him, that is, he can make stones out of the air and the water and the snow or anything. When the Sun's rays touched these stones, it was just like many bonfires. It almost blinded Unktomi and his friends. It was well for Unktomi to keep his mouth shut. The emaciated Sungila then appealed to Waceheska, "Oh, Father Waceheska, we are starving."

"Be patient, my child; you will not now starve; you are in your Father's house; you shall not want," he told him.

When they had been fed and rested, the Eagle, the master of ceremonies (Wayutan), came. Waceheska said to him, "Bring Unktomi and his party to me!" When they came, he told them to follow him. Then it was that Waceheska showed them what was in his house (teepee). First, he opened a door, where they found all the little insect people. They were beautifully dressed and very happy, enjoying themselves in work and play. They were the creeping insects. Then they were shown into another teepee—all the insects that fly. These, too, were busy and happy, and sang their wonderful songs. And so, they were shown all the little people of the world in the beautiful home of Eshnaicage and Waceheska. In this, they saw all the little butterflies, the little birds and the little animals who were not objectionable and dangerous. These were not subjected to the starvation caused by the great world blizzard.

After this, Waceheska took them into another part of the great teepee. There, they were shown all the chiefs of all the animals, from the least to the most dangerous and ferocious, in a great room, such as Eshnaicage and Waceheska wanted to save, who will live with his children in the ages to come. He had destroyed all the most dangerous and ill-shaped creatures, so they would not endanger the children of man.

When all these were shown, Waceheska told the Eagle to lead all the animal chiefs into one large room, and seated them on one side. Then, the Eagle was told to bring in the Man-people, that is, those creatures who were born with the image of Waceheska, although they too have animal blood in them. These were seated opposite the animals, that is, those who resembled the animals and only slightly resembled their father, Waceheska.

When all was done, Eshnaicage entered, leading his brother, Waceheska. The former took a high and beautiful seat in the room; his brother took one below him, above the people. Eshnaicage said to his brother Waceheska, "It is now time for you to lay before your children the laws and customs by which each class must be ruled henceforth."

During the gathering of the two classes, Unktomi modestly approached Waceheska, and said appealingly, "Brother Waceheska, where do I belong?"

"To the animals; you are Spider," he was told. So he has ever since been known as Unktomi, the Big Spider.

Waceheska then got up and addressed his children. "Listen, my beloved children of the Earth. I was brought to you by my brother Eshnaicage, to establish a new race on this Earth. In body, I have been raised by the original children of the Earth and the Sun, but my spirit is given by my brother Eshnaicage, by the command of the Great Spirit. But I have the blood of the Earth and the Sun, also. You are my children; you must obey my commandments."

Then he turned to the animal people and said, "I command that those of you who survived this great storm must live and produce children, but you are limited to your own tribe; you must have your own language and no other; you must not know the language of the Man-people. You will not intermarry with them; you are limited to your own country. You have promised to the Man-people, after the great war, that he may use your bodies when necessity demands. Those of you who are large and powerful must live only in the country I give you. You have been provided sufficiently for your living and self-protection. Obey the Sacred Law, Sacred Ritual."

Then he turned to the Man-people. "My beloved children, I have given my spirit and body to you. You have my image. I have given you more, the progressive mind. By this, you are permitted to use a free willpower. You shall make your own things for your comfort, convenience, and the happiness of your body and mind. You will have a clearer vision of the world things. The Spirit is given to all. You must respect the spirit of your animal brothers, and do not abuse their bodies wantonly. You will not know the language of the animal people. You must not intermarry with them. You may marry among all the tribes and nations of your own race, and learn each other's languages. By the Sacred Ritual, you may gather much knowledge of the things of the Earth. This world is full of knowledge and learning. You have the privilege to seek and learn. But you must not think yourself above the Sacred Ritual of the Great Spirit—that will destroy individuals as well as nations. Seek justice and purity for your body and mind. Then the spirit will be happy."

When he got through, Eshnaicage uttered a deep *A-ho-ho-ho,* which was heard all over the Earth. This great council was held after the snow was all melted, and the Earth was again covered with water, except the mountaintops, but they were far apart. Eshnaicage then decided to see all the people and the animals in their country, for they were scattered far and wide all over the Earth on isolated mountains, which were like islands.

For this purpose, he sent the Eagle and the Raven far north, for a big canoe. This big canoe was made of ice. It looked the same as glass. It was a beautiful canoe, almost like a big hill with cliffs. In this he took all the people who attended the great council to their respective homes. There were only a few people at each of these places, especially the Man-people, who were like the man as he is, in their form of body. They were good and innocent people. The animals, too, were especially selected. Man and animal occupied the same land, but did not talk the same language any more.

Eshnaicage sent the big Toad-Turtle-Reptile people either to the bottom of the Big Water or to some country where they will not bother the Man-people, except those tribes of them who were small; but they too were limited in their freedom.

During this trip, they came to a mountaintop, under the Sun's trail, where it was warmest, where they found some animals nearly like the Man-people, and some of the animals who were of the forbidden class. Waceheska told them, since they

· · ·

saved themselves, they must remain in the hottest part of the Earth, where man does not care to live, and must consider themselves animals, therefore, must have their own language. These were the Waunchalas, the imitators, the monkeys. Sometimes we called them Sunkawicasala, meaning the man dog.

Having completed their visit to all the people, Eshnaicage told each nation that his work for which he came was finished. He and Waceheska must then return to the Great Mystery, and then they will be required, still, to watch their children from the sky heaven. Eshnaicage will watch at night, and Waceheska must waken them up in the mornings and start them on their day's journey (life). Eshnaicage will then become the Evening Star, and Waceheska the Morning Star.

He told them that the Man-people must henceforth follow the example set by their father, Waceheska, that is, his spirit, body, and mind, to attain goodness and virtue.

After this, they departed in the big canoe upon the Big Water, and when they had reached the middle, the canoe appeared like a mountain on fire. Then, from it there arose a white (fleecy) cloud, floating skyward until it disappeared. Thus they returned to their spirits.

Since that far-off time, the Indians love the Morning and Evening Stars as their parents, whom the Great Spirit gave them. From these stories, the Indians formed their religion and customs, as Waceheska's parting words were:

"Come to me when you need me, but remember, you must rid yourselves of earthly things; come in spiritual simplicity, and in a child's attitude, and in truth."

Thus you see, my good children, that Waceheska was our father; he not only set the example of goodness and virtues with bravery, but he was the example—the model. He was not a preacher or propagandist, but teaches by example, brave and modest. He never claimed to be this and that—just let his life and character speak. Eshnaicage was the one who explained and commanded.

For these reasons, the Indian does not pray or sing in words, for words are cheap and a means of communication between human beings. When you appeal to them, which is to the Great Mystery himself, let your soul speak, not your human tongue; if you do the latter, you are speaking to human beings and not to the Spirit, or at least, not strongly. I want you to remember the difference between the spiritual prayer to the Great Mystery and the body prayer for the benefit of the body (physical prayer for material things). In the latter, prayer is directed to or through the Earth or Sun's spirits, which are invested in them by the Great Spirit, in the same way as the Soul Prayer is directed through Waceheska-Eshnaicage. The body prayer is imbued with selfishness, because it deals with temporal matter.

You must live in the open air and sun to accrue the spiritual strength. Silence and solitude help you much in this regard. For the Great Spirit dwells in all his creation, even if they are unconscious of Him.

In this manner, too, you convince yourself of these things, and you will obtain faith.

When all the human people and the animals were scattered on isolated mountain islands, all over the Earth, they were few, but selected. In time, these had forgotten that there were other peoples existing in other parts of the Earth, and they thought themselves the only people on the Earth. For they were on the mountain a long time before the waters of the Earth all returned to the Big Water. The waters that were left prisoners in places all over the Earth were the inland lakes. The trails between these two classes of waters, used by the waters which come from heaven to keep the Earth from drying, were the rivers of all sizes. In this way, the Earth was ever kept fresh and beautiful, and seeds can be planted for food for her children.

In time, there was much land where much vegetation grew up, even big forests. To these, both the man people and the animal people came down to live.

First, there were only a few saved on the mountain, but they had multiplied themselves very much, and when a tribe was too large, they separated, so that each tribe will have better land and planting. In time, these scattered over all the Earth. Many of them never met again. Some of these found the tribes of nations that came from other mountain tribes. But all have different languages and customs. As long as they have plenty of land for them all, they are all happy.

But after ages of time, many cultivated the land, more and more, and in order to do this, they captured many of the wild animals to help them in work and carrying their products for them, and when they had accumulated much of their product, they could not move about as they did at first.

In time, they established big camps and villages and lived there all the time. Also, in this manner, they built bigger teepees of wood and baked clay, and finally of stones. In these places they were increased very fast. At last, they even captured small tribes and made them work for them. They became powerful and made many wonderful things. But in their progress they became headstrong, because they made many things. They had many warriors and became very destructive to Nature and to man. They also became so selfish and careless of their spirits. The Great Mystery had destroyed many of that class of people since that far-off time, and started them anew each time.

From these experiences, many nations of the man people preferred to stay in the simple way of life.

In this way, our people started in our country. Our wise

men always taught their people to follow the simple life, and had the Sacred Ritual to guide them. Thus we lived here for ages when the white race came. Since then, our people have been forced to abandon our religion and philosophy, until now there are only a few of our great teachers left. Our young are forced to go to the white man's school, and there are now no children for us to teach. So, I am glad there are a few parents who still have faith in the old ways of training. In a few years more no Legend teachers will be left to teach the old Sacred Ritual.

My good children, I have finished the story.

— END —

the simple life, and had the Sacred Ritual to guide them. Thus, we lived here for ages when the white race came. Since then, our people have been forced to abandon our religion and philosophy, until now there are only a few of our great teachers ~~left~~ left. Our young are forced to go to the white man's school, and there are now, no children for us to teach. So, I am glad there are a few parents who still have faith in the old way of training. In a few years more no legend teacher will be left to teach the old Sacred Ritual.

My good children, I have finished the story.

END

Charles Alexander Eastman

(Ohiyesa)

The final page of the typescript.

PART 3
DAKOTA LEGACY

Charles Eastman and Mary Eastman Faribault.

Remembering Relatives

YVONNE WYNDE

THIS IS ABOUT MY MEMORIES OF MY CLOSE RELATIVES
who knew Charles Alexander Eastman, the brother of my
great-grandfather, and how his many books about the Dakota
people have provided needed information about life in the
nineteenth century. I lived at Old Agency on the Sisseton
Wahpeton Oyate's Lake Traverse Reservation during his lifetime, but I was too young to recall his visits here, where his
sister and brother and many nieces and nephews lived. Many
who were there gained knowledge regarding the Dakota ways
in kinship, principles, and morals during that period in Dakota
history—knowledge that did not come from classroom settings. Charles Eastman's family influenced the person he
became.

I first came to know about the Eastman family, which was
a large family, when I was very young, in the 1930s. Since many
were deceased, I learned of them through my father's stories

that he often related. The people of whom I speak are the children of Nancy Eastman and TaWakanHdiOta, His Many Lightnings, who was later named Jacob Eastman. Nancy and Jacob had five children. In order of births they were Mary Eastman (TipiWakanwin, Sacred Lodge, 1847–1937, Mrs. David Faribault Jr.), John Eastman, David Eastman (TateIyotanna, Great Wind, 1848–1918, my great-grandfather), James Eastman, and Charles Eastman. They were young in 1862, during the Dakota–US War in Minnesota. Charles Eastman wrote in *Indian Boyhood* that he was four when his family left the devastation of that place and period.

I listened to stories of that time in Dakota history from both sides of my family. On my mother's side, I knew my great-grandmother, Kunsi (TiyoMazawin, Iron Door, 1858–1947), who was about the same age as Charles Eastman when she and her mother (WakanIyotakawin, Sits Above, 1837–1923) fled Minnesota and settled at Enemy Swim Lake in what is now northeastern South Dakota. This was prior to the establishment of the Sisseton Wahpeton Lake Traverse Reservation in 1867. I heard horrific stories from my father and elders about that time.

This disruption of their lives caused them to fear being captured and incarcerated. This eventually happened, even to old men and young women, as Dakota people experienced at Fort Snelling. Diseases such as measles, tuberculosis, and trachoma, to name a few, which were spread by the white people among the Dakota, also had severe detrimental effects.

After the Dakota War of 1862, many Dakota people fled Minnesota to keep their families safe, and they never returned. In 1863, only one year after the Dakota–US War, Congress passed a law to remove all Dakota people from the state of

Minnesota. This included people and bands, whether or not they were involved in the fighting. This was the Removal Act of 1863. The major thrust for this law was to get more land, some of the richest in the country, from Native Americans and to continue with genocidal motives.

Sovereignty was another issue. The Dakota people were a sovereign nation. The question is this: how can one nation legally and culturally remove language and culture from another nation, through forced education measures and laws?

In 1883, twenty-one years after the war of 1862, the secretary of the Interior decreed the Code of Indian Offenses, and the Congress passed laws to enforce it. The Dakota people realized the primary motive of these laws was to further "civilization" policies. Dakota people were not to practice their religion or customs. If they violated the Code of Indian Offenses, they were punished by the Court of Indian Offenses. But stopping the practice of Native religions became a violation of the people's First Amendment rights in 1924, when they became United States citizens. How had these laws affected the life of Charles Eastman? He married a white woman, but this union did not assure him safety from racism. When he uncovered corruption as a physician at Pine Ridge, he lost his employment there. Nor did it assure him a successful career as a physician in the white community, when he and his wife moved to St. Paul and then to New Hampshire.

The Eastman Compound

My paternal grandmother, Mary Eastman Wynde (1882–1918), was a genteel woman who had many refinements in the operation of her household. She was active in the Goodwill Presbyterian

Church. Her husband, Theodore Wynde, was a farm laborer and worked for the Sisseton Wahpeton farm. But my grandmother did not live to see her children reach adulthood. She died, leaving motherless my father, Lawrence Edward Wynde (Catan, fourth-born son, 1907–1967), an eleven-year-old; his sisters, Ramona (Winona) and Olive; and his brother, Theodore Jr. Their father died at a relatively young age also.

It was Mary Eastman Faribault, the older sister of David and Charles Eastman, who took her brother's grandchildren into her household at Old Agency. My father's stories showed that he was very close to her. I was born in her house, and she died when I was five years old. Sadly, I do not have recollections of her, only of her house and the stories my father told about her.

Mary Eastman, who was born in 1847, had married David Faribault Jr. (WakanHdi Topa, Four Lightnings, 1843–1913) in 1861, one year before the outbreak in Minnesota. One year after the outbreak, she was imprisoned at Fort Snelling while still an adolescent. Her freedom was taken away from her as she was transported by boat down the Mississippi River to St. Louis and up the Missouri River to Crow Creek, where she lived in a tent for three years. She went to Santee, Nebraska, for two years; then to Flandreau, South Dakota, where her father and other members of the family lived; and then settled in Sisseton at Old Agency, where she received a land allotment. Tent living at Crow Creek and Santee in extreme heat and unbearable winters was not conducive to healthy child rearing. Many of her children died in early childhood. Despite these hardships, she was proper in her life and caring to her younger relatives. She had a house built, cultivated gardens, and raised livestock.

*

I remember being in Mary Eastman Faribault's house just one time. It happened in my early adolescent years, ten years after her death. One rainy summer day, my brother and I rode horseback through a pasture which led past Mary Eastman Faribault's house. I explained to him that this house was where our father spent many years of his life and where I was born. It was a two-story house that appeared intact and had no broken windows, but needed paint, as it must have been vacant since her death. I decided to investigate the house, as I heard so many stories about it.

As we approached the front door, I saw a World War I soldier's jacket on the porch floor in front of the doorway. The door was unlocked, and it opened to a foyer that led to a stairway. There were rooms on each side of the foyer. On the left were the front room and the dining room, separated by doors that slid into the walls. I looked for this feature, as I had heard about it. I saw the chandelier that I heard about also. A kitchen with a large woodstove was next. I did not go into the room on the east side of the foyer, as I knew it was Mary Eastman Faribault's room. We crept up the stairway to the second floor and stood at the first room at the head of the stairs. Through the open doorway I saw a large trunk, filled to the top with papers and letters. There was a desk and chair in the room also.

We were in the house fewer than ten minutes when we suddenly heard a very loud thumping. We turned and raced out of the house, then continued on our way. Later we thought that knocking sound was my brother's dog, scratching himself. We never went back to the house. Many years later, I thought that I should have told my father about the trunk and its contents. But it was much too late, as the house had been razed.

Mary Eastman Faribault's husband, David Faribault Jr., also lived in this house for about thirty years. He, too, was imprisoned for three years after the war in 1862. While a prisoner in Davenport, Iowa, as a very young person, he wrote letters to Henry Sibley, the leader of Minnesota's military forces. One of his letters was published in *The Dakota Prisoner of War Letters*, translated by Clifford Canku and Michael Simon. I remembered a relative, Solomon Faribault, who spent time with my father and was at our house occasionally. He was the only Faribault that I remember.

Mary and David had many children, and according to probate records only four survived to adulthood: Solomon, David, Lucinda, and Viola. However, they all died before their parents did.

Mary Eastman Faribault and her husband and children spoke Dakota as their first language. Her house with its many rooms showed that she was a progressive woman. She was not colonized but saw survival through her farm business and remained a Dakota woman. She expressed her life through Dakota values and customs.

The two-story house of my great-grandfather David Eastman (Charles's brother) stood about half a mile east of our house. There was a barn, a chicken coop, and an old artesian well with a spout that ran slowly and constantly into a concrete trough. A creek ran through the large pasture. It swept through our pasture, running eastward into the Peever Slough. Cottonwood trees framed three sides of the farmyard, with an opening to the south. A railroad track between Milbank and Sisseton lay about half a mile to the east. David's son Alexander had a farm near his place. Gardens and farm animals were raised at this home. Benny Faribault had a homestead nearby. Rebecca Eastman inherited property close by. David Faribault also had property "near the railroad track near David Eastman's place," according to records.

There was a story that when a Dakota man was to be lynched by the local white farmers, a secret meeting of elderly Dakota men took place at David Eastman's house to avert this action. The meeting was held during the night. Lamps were not lit. The only flickering light came from a wood-stove. The man was rescued from the Sisseton courthouse jail during the night and taken across the border to Browns Valley, Minnesota.

It was in November in 1937 when Mary Eastman Faribault walked three miles from her home to the home of her close friend Capena. She became disoriented and was lost during the night in a nearby cornfield. Weakened by the freezing weather, she was found the next morning by a neighbor who saw an unfamiliar object in the harvested field. She was taken to the local hospital and died there at age ninety. My father became very angry at her caretaker and threatened him. She was buried at the Goodwill Presbyterian cemetery in Agency. Years later, in 1967, my father was buried next to her grave.

To this day in 2021, Capena's house is still standing. A long row of lilac bushes grows on the east side of her house, hiding it from view. These events occurred during my lifetime.

I grew up on the Eastman Compound on the property my father inherited from Mary Eastman Wynde. I found broken shards of china where she had lived and thick lavender glass that may have been from a stained glass window. I found a horseshoe near the place where a barn once stood. Evidence of a root cellar indicated gardening. At the creek running through this property, I learned not to fear water and to swim. The creek banks were thick with trees: cottonwoods, box elders, willows;

the shrubs are chokecherry, plums, and gooseberry. This land was very fertile, excellent for gardening and farming. All of the relatives of that era spoke the Dakota language as their first language, and many spoke English well. This is where I learned of the incarceration of family members at Fort Snelling, including Mary Eastman Faribault.

I realized as an adult that my father's friends were also his close relatives. These people, I knew, were very respectful of each other. David Eastman's adult grandchildren frequently came to the Eastman Compound. King Jones, who trapped near our house, was the son of Agnes Eastman Jones. David Marks was the son of Rebecca Eastman. These relatives were kindly and helped each other during the Great Depression and at other crucial times. Close relationships that I saw as a child are no longer visible today. Presently, many no longer know their ancestry or who their close relatives are—and in fact have intermarried with their relatives. Preventing marriage with relatives was a natural law of the Dakota people. This was one of the reasons for the kinship system that had ruled the Dakota people's way of life.

I asked my mother if she knew Charles Eastman. She answered, "I knew Charlie." I imagined that he must have ridden a horse or driven a buggy to visit his brother, David, next door, or his niece (and my grandmother) Mary Eastman Wynde. Charles Eastman worked for a short period at the Lake Traverse Reservation, as he was bilingual. Most of the adults at Sisseton spoke Dakota as their first language, and some did not speak the English language. During that time, interpreters worked at the local Bureau of Indian Affairs office. Charles notified people of the government's regulations, such as not recognizing multiple partners in marriage. Any violation of the Code of Indian

Offenses was punished by the Court of Indian Offenses. Often a Dakota was arrested, and the people found out later what the offense consisted of. It was a trying time to leave old traditions and convert to the government's expectations.

As a young child in Canada, Charles Eastman learned about the Dakota traditions that made him a man of integrity, according to the ways of his paternal grandmother and uncles. His grandmother wanted him to become a medicine man to know the healing plants and ceremonies that were vital to healthy living. He chose to attend the white man's educational institutions and become a physician. She influenced his spirituality by teaching him about Wakan Tanka, the Great Mystery. "Religion was the basis of all Indian training," writes Charles Eastman.

In the traditional Dakota way, families should have no more than four children. Children were known by birth-order names until they received their own name. In order of birth, for the girls, the names were Winona, Hapan, Hopstin, and Wanske. For the boys, it was Caske, Hepan, Hepi, and Catan. A first-born child would be called Winona if a girl and Caske if a boy. There could not be a Winona and a Caske in the same family, as the names applied to the first-born only. The fifth child was called Hake, the last one. Charles Eastman referred to himself as Hakada, or the pitiful last. Pitiful is not part of the meaning of the word *Hake*.

In the 1930s Charles and his sister, Mary, attempted to locate the grave of their mother, who was buried at the Lower Sioux Indian Community, with no success.

When I learned of Charles Eastman as an author from my mother and aunt, I sought out his books in used bookstores. As I read them, they corroborated the legends I heard from my elders. I was appalled that very few people knew of his books and they were not used in schools. I took many of his books to Roger Buffalohead, who was a professor at the University of Minnesota. Later, I began to see reprints of Charles Eastman's books.

Charles Eastman's many published books revealed commitments to ceremonies as he describes the origin and the way they were performed. He tells of the important elders he encountered as a child: his great-grandfather Mahpiya Wicasta (Cloud Man); Wabasha (Red Hat or Red Banner); and Maka To (Blue Earth), leaders we should know in history. He describes the child-rearing patterns established for centuries, when raising honorable men and women was the ultimate goal.

He reveals the honorable relationship the Dakota people had with animals and land. His books on chiefs who lived during his lifetime give us a closer view of them. The history of these leaders belonged in teachings, and he describes the stature of the Dakota during that era. His writing gives an insight into a proper diet to encourage a healthy lifestyle.

The Creation Stories Today

The creation stories that Charles Eastman has preserved in this book show laws and customs that are still known and practiced in my community. Among these are child-rearing methods, treatment of elders, philosophical teachings, and stories of ceremonies and food.

Storytelling was the linkage to times past. It taught morals, laws, and customs while it promoted reasoning. I recall hearing creation stories at the home of Kunsi, my maternal great-grandmother. John T. Keeble, her close relative, had also escaped Minnesota territory at about the same time and age as she did.

Once when he stayed overnight at Kunsi's home, he told these stories and told us to acknowledge his tales by responding to his pauses, with girls saying "Han" and boys saying "Hau." This continued until no children spoke, and the storytelling ended for the night.

My parents were also storytellers. They told stories of Unktomi (Spider) and Iya (Eayah, Greedy Eater). We heard "Unktomi and His Bundle of Songs" and other animal stories based on Unktomi's antics. My mother told the story of the woman mud turtle that was performing a woman's traditional dance in an upright position. My mother added the sound that turtles supposedly made. She said she wished that she remembered all the ancient stories told to her.

Proper behavior was enforced in families and taught from early childhood. My great-grandmother was the matriarch, and I heard her scold grown men. Lullabies (page 37) were an integral part of early child rearing. Soothing and comforting children was evident. *Abu* (sleep) may be the first word learned by infants. As the legends show, many woman relatives are responsible for caring for and teaching children (pages 79, 81). In Dakota households, it is sometimes difficult to identify the mother, as all of the women are caretakers.

As a child grows, others help with instruction. In these legends, Isna Icage (phonetic spelling Eshnaicage, Grew Alone) was responsible for teaching his little brother, who eventually received the name Wacehin Ska (phonetic spelling Wacheska, White Feather or White Eagle Tail Feathers), to be of good character. He received the help of the eagle, who taught self-control and the meaning of hardship; the grizzly bear, who showed him the need for strength and bravery and shared his medicinal properties with him; and others. The animals of the deep were of no help to Wacehin Ska. Most of these stories that have been carried on today through the Itunkakan stories were not true tales and were teachings for children.

Unktomi occasionally reintroduces ancient laws that are prevalent today. One example is the respect shown to elders (page 49). Because of their age and wisdom, elders are allowed to speak at public occasions. Today this custom still applies. Elders may speak to councils whenever they wish and on whatever topic they choose. Elders do not have to publicly recognize anyone; others must show respect to them.

Unktomi's mourning customs (page 51) are still carried on by those who know the old ways—for instance, cutting hair or letting hair that was usually tightly braided hang loose. I heard a family story of relatives who were missing and thought to have died in a blizzard. When the relatives arrived safely home, family members had cut their hair in mourning. Slashing arms was practiced in ancient times, but this was not common. Men singing dirges was last heard of during the early part of the past century. I have not experienced this, but my mother had and spoke about it.

Many ceremonies are performed in this community. Inipi lodges (page 62) are not an uncommon sight at local family homes. Teaching ceremonial songs has been ongoing since ancient times. Many families have their own pipestone pipes (page 124) that they use in their ceremonies. Most tribes revere eagle feathers, and their presentation is significant; the giving of an eagle feather for noble deeds continues today (page 106). Fasting and prayers are continual events (pages 62, 64, 106, 122). Types of prayers (pages 64, 144) were known; prayers of the spirit were stronger than praying for material items.

Dance was an important ritual among the Dakota people

that came from ancient times (page 62). It has evolved to many types of dances for men and women. Ancient songs and current songs were part of the dances. Drums, societies, and sacred bundles are contemporary items written about in Eastman's manuscript (pages 62, 63, 69). Concepts of progressive minds, free will, silence, and solitude are evident today (page 141).

The legends tell of the origins of the morning and evening stars (page 143). My mother told me that her grandmother and great-grandmother awoke when the morning star arose. They began the day with a prayer saying that Wakan Tanka was good to them as he brought them to another day. I recently heard this same prayer at a public event. These people of the older generation spoke of the morning star, the evening star, and the constellations as links to the creation stories. One evening I heard my great-grandmother comment about the position of the star dipper as kaptan, or emptied.

Dakota people devised methods to practice medicine (pages 58–60). Only certain honorable people were taught about medicinal plants, as this could be a dangerous practice—as it is in the modern world.

Food, the life-giving element, was utmost in the ways of Dakota people. Serving food was part of almost every ceremony, except in the case of Sun Dancers, who fast. Certain plants grew on the prairies, and children were taught to identify them in various seasons of growth and to learn to harvest and preserve food. Just as in the legends (page 134), corn and tobacco are planted and then stored when the growing season has passed.

The legends tell of a great destruction and later restoration (page 134). What implications does this have for today's situation when growing food? Unfortunately, because of modern agricultural practices, many plants, foods, and medicines have been destroyed. It is difficult to find the potatoes, prairie turnips, and wild onions on the prairies that once sustained tribes.

Juneberry shrubs as well as chokecherry and plum shrubs are also being affected, and many have died. Another concern is the decimation of the wild rose shrub. As the legends warn (page 113), the Medicine people "thought they were entitled to know even the secrets of the Great Mystery. This will always be so, and such people will destroy themselves in the end. They become destructive of Nature, and since they are part of that Nature, they destroy themselves."

Throughout, the legends tell of the teaching of the Great Spirit and show government entities such as councils and protective bodies such as warriors. Women had a responsibility in government, as one time they proposed no more war (page 125).

With the passage of time, customs of the Dakota people are changing. Learning the origin of ancient laws and customs is crucial. The influences of ancient Dakota life still exist among younger Dakota tribal members, even though they may not recognize the origin of the teachings. This is a very important reason to publish this book.

In books Eastman authored, we learn that the Dakota people revered their way of life, one that sustained them for centuries. The organization of life in the tiyospaye, or community, provided for peaceful living. His stories also reveal that all tribes should negotiate and discuss ways for peaceful living together. His books provide a view of the richness of life that many no longer remember or promote. Charles Eastman based his knowledge on his reality in living the Dakota way. Later, assimilation caused many ceremonies and customs to be performed surreptitiously. I may not remember seeing Charles Eastman, but I lived during his lifetime and near his siblings. I have great appreciation and gratitude for his writings.

Charles Alexander Eastman.

Ohiyesa:
From the Sacred Earth of the
Oceti Sakowin, a Literary Tradition

GABRIELLE TATEYUSKANSKAN

ARTISTS HAVE THE DIFFICULT ROLE OF REFLECTION; THEY hold the mirror for us to look at ourselves. In spite of the colonial settler attitude toward the first people of this continent, Ohiyesa or Charles Eastman persevered with his art as a writer. While working on his manuscript "The Sioux Creation Legend," he also experienced issues with his health; this is documented in his January 14, 1935, letter to H. M. Hitchcock.[1] He states, "I have not been as strong as usual and have neglected much of my research work in history of the earlier periods in America." His health distress slowed but did not prevent him from ongoing work, until he journeyed on from this earth on January 8, 1939. At the time, this loss deprived the Dakota Oyate or Nation, and a larger public audience, of the completed published work of this manuscript, of the man as an artist and teacher.

Art bears witness to and expresses what it means to be human. The artist is an important resource to his community, his country, and the larger world. Struggling for his art as Ohiyesa did, he overcame the barrier of achieving an education as a Dakota first-language speaker to attend and graduate from Dartmouth College, earning a bachelor of letters degree with honors. Ohiyesa completed his medical studies at Boston College to become a physician. He strived against racism and unscrupulous federal employees to establish himself in the medical profession as a doctor. As a writer, he did persevere to author and publish several books based on his Dakota heritage. He also had to defend his right to his Dakota viewpoint and authorship. There are still efforts to denigrate his works of art by critics outside of Dakota culture. Skeptical critiques speculate on how much of his work is his own or claim it is that of his wife, Elaine Goodale Eastman. This skepticism is an attempt to diminish the preeminence of his authority as an author in the field of Dakota literature.

Ohiyesa was born a citizen of the Oyate; Indigenous people did not become American citizens until Congress enacted the Indian Citizenship Act on June 2, 1924. The Oyate is a confederacy that consists of the Oceti Sakowin or Seven Council Fires. This is the traditional political organization. The bands include the Bdewakantunwan, Sissetunwan, Wahpekute, and Wahpetunwan. These bands also comprise the Isanyati or the Dakota dialect speakers. There are also the Nakota speakers, who are the Ihanktunwan and Ihanktunwanna. Included in the alliance are the Titunwan or the Lakota dialect speakers that are further organized into seven subgroups.

For Ohiyesa, it must have been a difficult challenge to confront the power and privilege of American society through his written narratives. His storylines expressed the truth of what it meant to be Dakota, as the Dakota perspective is distinct and not always easy for those outside the culture to comprehend. Ohiyesa documented the world as it was during his era and created a vision of what it could be. His speeches and written work challenge many of the racist beliefs held by American society during his lifetime and today. America not only ignored the value of Dakota culture, education systems, and literary traditions, it also outlawed many aspects of them.

Racism is found in the very foundation of America, in opposition to the proclaimed inalienable ideals of equality, rights, and freedoms defined in the US Constitution. The ethnocentric American societal attitude falsely claims the original people of this continent are inferior human beings.

This perception demeaned Indigenous people, allowing for a lapse of conscience to enable exploitation. Therefore, America did not respect the sovereignty of Indigenous nations or the human rights of their citizens. American society as a powerful political force acted with impunity. This outlook led to the immoral actions of land theft, cultural suppression, persecution, racial violence, and attempted extermination of the original people of this continent. Ohiyesa witnessed and addressed these harms in his writing and speeches and through his activism as a member of the Society of American Indians. He spoke out about the racial oppression, injustice, and harms he observed in his lifetime.

Life was precarious and turbulent for the Dakota Oyate during non-Indigenous settler occupation of Dakota makoce or aboriginal territory. The tiwahe or family members of Ohiyesa experienced the trauma of incarceration, exile, bounties, pursuit by citizen militia, and persecution from military campaigns. As a young child, he and his family were a part of the traumatic flight from Dakota makoce during the Dakota–US War of 1862. Ohiyesa experienced the hardship of living as a refugee in Canada with his brother Catan or James Eastman, his paternal uncle Pejuta Wakan, and Unchida, his paternal grandmother.

Ohiyesa's father, Ta Wakanhdi Ota or Jacob His Many Light-nings Eastman, survived harsh conditions as a prisoner of war at Camp McClellan in Davenport, Iowa. Ohiyesa's brothers Hepan Mahpiya Wakankidan or John Eastman and Hepi Tatei-yotanna or David Eastman had also suffered as prisoners in Iowa. Winona Tipi Wakan Win or Mary Eastman Faribault, his sister, endured the horrific conditions of imprisonment in a concentration camp located at Fort Snelling in Minnesota. In the spring of 1863 she was a part of the forced exile of the Dakota from Minnesota to confinement at Crow Creek, South Dakota. As a physician, Ohiyesa provided medical treatment to the massacre survivors who were members of the Tatanka Iyotake Oyate and the Upan Gleska Oyate—Sitting Bull's and Spotted Elk's people—at Wounded Knee Creek on December 29, 1890.

As a writer, Ohiyesa contributed to the difficult work of building a pathway for the Oyate away from the dishearten-ing situation of colonization toward repair of the wounds from brutal non-Indigenous settler occupation. He challenged the race-based practices of subordination permitted by laws and facilitated by educational institutions in American society. He promoted Dakota history as a part of American history and integral to understanding the past, present, and future of this country. His writing was an attempt at a mutual exchange of ideas, fostering understanding of another language, a different cultural perspective, and an additional literary tradition.

Ohiyesa would have been mindful of race-based assimilation policies, also referred to as the civilization codes—policies such as the Civilization Fund Act of March 3, 1819, and the Dawes Act of February 8, 1887, to assimilate the original people away from their ancient heritage and into the culture of American society. During his lifetime, he was a witness to lethal racial violence and harms from injustices. His awareness of intolerant societal attitudes and of the impact of harms and oppressive policies would have made him cautious in writing about Dakota culture and spiritual matters. In 1883 the US Congress passed legislation establishing the Code of Indian Offenses and the Court of Indian Offenses. The purpose of these codes and courts was to make the practice of Indigenous culture and spirituality illegal. The repercussions for being found in violation of these policies could be extremely harsh. The first people were intimidated through starvation by having their annuities taken away, threatened by having their children forcibly taken to boarding schools far from their home communities, and silenced by confinement in jails and prisons.

The literary inheritance of the Oyate has been negatively affected by the racism of colonial settler society. These repressive tactics have deprived many Dakota of their ancestral literature. The policies of the assimilation era prevented the continuous teaching of the Dakota language, culture, spirituality, and history of the Oyate. The harmful misguided statement of Richard H. Pratt, the founder of Carlisle Indian Industrial Institute, one of the first federal boarding schools, established in 1879, documents this oppressive attitude. Pratt is noted for the phrase "Kill the Indian in him, save the man." This assertion is an example of the racial intolerance toward Indigenous people that has existed in American education systems and the culture of its society for decades.

In 1898 legislation established the Hiawatha Insane Asylum for Indians. This institution was located in Canton, South Dakota. The primary purpose of this asylum was to detain Indigenous people who refused to stop the practice of their traditional cultural and spiritual lifeways. The institution began incarcerating individuals in January 1903. The administrators and staff lacked training in behavioral health, which led to abuses within

the institution. Approximately 121 people died while being punished for resistance and enduring severe medical neglect; they are
buried at the asylum. A federal investigation revealed that most
of those who were held in this facility did not have a mental health
diagnosis and suffered under extreme, inhumane conditions. The
documented severe harms resulted in the institution being closed
in 1934 by Commissioner of Indian Affairs John Collier.[2] Thus,
serious consequences for practicing the traditional culture and
spirituality were harsh realities. Justifiable fear can be a powerful
barrier to resistance; Ohiyesa demonstrated fortitude in applying
his academic training to promote understanding and social justice for the Oceti Sakowin in the hope the Oyate could achieve
equal standing in American society.

A brutal American society denied the original people the
consolation of their spiritual lifeways. Many of the traditional
spiritual practices went underground to provide the necessary ceremonial space to pray, offer benevolence, and support
restoration from hurts and healing. Spiritual freedom for the
original people would not be protected until the passage of the
American Indian Religious Freedom Act in 1978. It was a cou-
rageous act of resistance to demonstrate civil disobedience by
disregarding the Code of Indian Offenses. Ohiyesa would have
carefully taken into consideration the intolerance of American
society during his time and weighed the possibility of negative
outcomes because of the subject matter of this manuscript. He
persevered as a writer and did not allow racism or the cultural
erasure of assimilationist policies to stifle his work.

The role of an artist is essential to helping facilitate the communication of ideas in any society. Through his manuscript, Ohiyesa created a window for readers to view the land-based oral
tradition of the Oceti Sakowin in a written form. He makes it possible to discover a diverse perspective and find what hasn't been
written about before. In Dakota culture, the storytellers play a

significant part in the early instruction of wakanheja or children. Through vivid oral accounts, children were taught to know their ancestors, to visualize a future earth of wisdom, and to be humane; they learned to honor the kinship system by being good relatives. This education structure ensured Indigenous knowledge of the Oyate would be transmitted to succeeding generations.

Storytelling was a typical part of an early childhood education, as well as a sophisticated performance art. The stories were complex and an expressive way to teach young people the beliefs, values, societal standards, and spiritual ways of the people. The oral tradition nurtures the spiritual imagination of the Oyate. The oral accounts emphasize the important ideal that all life is sacred. The stories impart to children a growing awareness of the sanctity of living beings that is expressed by the phrase "Mitakuye owasin" or "All my relatives." The elders of the community who had a lifetime of experience, Indigenous knowledge, and wisdom were the living libraries of the culture. They also had exemplary memory skills. Those who excelled at the art of telling oral narratives could repeat information verbatim. This skill ensured that important cultural teachings were imparted to their young audience exactly as they were meant to be spoken. Most importantly, these narratives are a direct connection to Dakota knowledge carried by the ancestors who came before us.

Ehanna, or long ago, it was the role of the grandparents to be the first teachers to their takoja or grandchildren. A common method for imparting knowledge was through oral narratives. In Dakota communities, the stories were told during the waniyetu or winter months. Children competed to be the first to ask the best storyteller of the community to their tipi for an evening meal and afterward the much-anticipated time of storytelling.

After the evening meal was finished, the family got comfortable, ready to listen to their guest. The best storytellers reenacted parts of the story. They mimicked the sounds of animals or the voices of the individuals speaking in the narrative. Storytellers also used their bodies in expressive and animated ways to imitate their characters. Through creative and imaginative drama, they depicted the personalities of animals, birds, people, and spiritual entities contained in the story.

At the beginning of the narrative, the storyteller explained to their young audience that there would be periodic pauses during the telling of the story. The young relatives were told the purpose of this pause: it was a test to see how attentive they were. During this break in the story, the wicinyanna or young girls were instructed to say the female affirmation, "han." The hoksina or young boys were told to say in male gender speech, "hau." The storyteller would continue with the story until there was no longer a response to the pause in the telling, meaning the children had all fallen asleep. If the story had not been completed, the rest of the oral narrative could be continued at another evening of storytelling. This manuscript by Ohiyesa is a valuable contribution to literature and necessary to continue the transmission of ancestral knowledge imparted by the oral tradition of the Oceti Sakowin through a contemporary written art form.

Tateiyotanna or David Eastman was one of Ohiyesa's older brothers and is my unkanna sampa, my great-great-grandfather. He resided with his tiyospaye or extended family on the Lake Traverse Reservation, established in 1867 in northeastern South Dakota. The immediate family members of Tateiyotanna, after their release from imprisonment, searched to find their relatives and reunite the tiwahe. Their father Ta Wakanhdi Ota, after his release from Camp McClellan, acquired a 160-acre homestead in the community of Flandreau, South Dakota, in 1868. His home is located approximately 125 miles south of the Lake Traverse Reservation. Their brother Mahpiya Wakankidan also lived in the community of Flandreau and later joined his two siblings on the Lake

Traverse Reservation, where he became the minister of Tawacin Waste or Goodwill Presbyterian Church, located at Old Agency.

The Tateiyotanna tiyospaye, like other Dakota tiyospaye, was looking for a safe haven to restore their lives and renew their spirits from the adversity and persecution they had experienced. Under the General Allotment Act of 1887, women received allotments on the Lake Traverse Reservation. Tipi Wakan Win somehow survived the extreme difficulties of imprisonment at Crow Creek. She was released from confinement, traveled to Santee, Nebraska, and with determination reached her father's home at Flandreau, South Dakota. From there, Tipi Wakan Win went to the Sisseton Agency, where she was allotted land near her brother Tateiyotanna. Several members of their tiyospaye were also allotted lands east of the Sisseton Agency near an area now called Old Agency Village. The tiyospaye was fortunate to have received allotments of good fertile cropland that were located in proximity to each other. This enabled the family to provide support to one another and repair the disruption of family life caused by the Dakota–US War of 1862 and the Dakota exile from their beloved ancient homeland.

The physical, cultural, and spiritual freedoms the Dakota Oyate had once known were still in the people's living memory. The Dakota language, the land, kinship, and spirituality are the cultural foundations of the Oyate. The Tateiyotanna tiyospaye continued to speak the Dakota language. Their families kept alive the language of the original people of Dakota makoce. Living close together also provided the members of the tiyospaye the opportunity to maintain the social structure of the kinship system. They became agriculture producers, shared land resources, and further retained their cultural identity by following the Dakota economic tradition of collective farming to support their families. Their progressive lifestyle was in opposition to the intent of the Dawes Act, which was to assimilate the original people away from their culture of origin.

The elders in my family enjoyed and excelled at the traditional art of storytelling. They related to their takoja the narratives from the oral tradition, tribal history, and family stories. The ancestors of the Oyate have lived with and nurtured Dakota makoce from time immemorial. The accounts from the oral tradition are based on an ancient relationship with sacred earth and explain the cosmology of the Oceti Sakowin. For the Oyate, spirituality is vital to identity and to understanding the sanctity of Dakota makoce. I was fortunate to have experienced and learned Dakota narratives from my relatives. Our family members created a learning environment that continuously nurtured our Dakota upbringing. My mother took an active interest in our education and visited many used bookstores during my childhood, collecting the work of our relative, Ohiyesa. My siblings and I enjoyed literature; the collected works by Ohiyesa were available to us in our home, and we had the opportunity to read his books. His image is in many family photo albums and displayed in the homes of my relatives. I did ask Kunsi, my grandmother, if she had known Ohiyesa. She replied, "Charlie, oh yes." Kunsi explained to my siblings and me that Ohiyesa spoke the Dakota language when he interacted with the Dakota public and relatives. He remains a familiar figure in the family, the tiyospaye, and the Dakota community.

It was Kunsi, elder relatives, and my mother who took my siblings and me to the physical locations on the Dakota landscape where family history, the history of the Oyate, the star maps, and the settings from oral narratives occurred. My relatives also promoted our inner spiritual life by explaining how the Dakota cosmology that is conveyed in the oral accounts and ancient sacred places correlates to Dakota values practiced in ceremonial life.

Ceremony grounds the people to sacred earth with a responsibility as caretakers, guardians, and stewards who reside on a shared landscape with a community of other living beings and spiritual entities. We were introduced to spiritual symbolism beginning with a design pattern that resembles the shape of an hourglass. This symbol relates that what is in the spiritual universe is mirrored onto the physical earth. This intimate understanding of the Dakota place in the cosmos is communicated to young people through sacred places, Dakota star knowledge, and the creation narratives. The arts of the Dakota are intertwined with spirituality, and teaching values to young people happens through the vibrant art of storytelling, the mystery of physical altars on the earth, and the making of beautiful ceremonial accoutrements.

From childhood, I was inspired by the art of storytelling and the written word. I was also conscious from my own experience that intolerance prevented books written by Indigenous authors from being available in American classrooms and in school and public libraries. American society has a legacy of dismissing Dakota knowledge systems that are a valuable and complex part of the Oyate culture. When I attended high school at the Institute of American Indian Arts in Santa Fe, New Mexico, I had the chance to read the works of many Indigenous authors. I was astonished at the number of written works from the Oceti Sakowin and other Indigenous nations. As students, we realized something had been profoundly missing in our formal education. We found a place where what it meant to be a member of the original people of this continent was a part of the academic discourse. The literary canon we were introduced to included narratives of the cultural reality of how we lived our everyday lives. I was inspired by the words of these authors and spent many hours in the library, motivated by these books. I was encouraged by my instructors, who were Indigenous, many of them published authors, to continue my study of the literature of the Oyate. They emphasized the necessity of including the many literary voices of the original people as valued contributors to the literature of the world.

It is vital to the Oyate that the oral narratives Ohiyesa has translated and transcribed into the written word are made available, although the sounds and visual effect of the spoken word are lost in the written versions of the accounts. The written words are still valuable for the insights provided by Ohiyesa as someone who was raised in Dakota lifeways. His work is crucial to the sustained transmission of Dakota knowledge to a new generation. The people have endured oppression, suffered from atrocities, and been disheartened by many losses. What we cannot survive is the absence of our artistic expressions.

In this country, there is a difference between stated principles, moral attention, and the capacity for ethical action. Dakota communities suffer today from the historical legacy of land theft, racial oppression, deadly violence, and American societal indifference to these harms, which has resulted in many social ills for the Oyate up to the twenty-first century. For societal health, America must examine the fraught relationship it has with the original people of this continent. Works of art can serve the public interest as they can inform and provide the opportunity for contemplation and discussion of difficult subject matter.

During the era of the Civil Rights movement of the 1960s, through their dedicated work, Dakota and other Indigenous scholars such as Elizabeth Cook-Lynn, Patricia Locke, Vine Deloria Jr., Roger Buffalohead, and many others challenged the academy to include Native Studies as a serious area of academic discipline. These academics made the decisions about what literature should be included in this field of study. My mother, Yvonne Wynde, introduced the out-of-print published writing of Ohiyesa to her colleagues in the field of education. The works of Ohiyesa were then nurtured, valued, and supported by Indigenous scholars in the universities. As a respected Dakota author, he is regarded for his documentation of the experiences of the Oyate during a tumultuous era of American history. He provides perspective on the severity of the discrimination, oppression, and harms the Oyate endured due to non-Indigenous settler occupation of Dakota makoce. This historical context makes available an important framework to examine the impact of colonization on the Dakota literary tradition, to learn or relearn hard truths, and to create understanding. The significant work of those academics in Native Studies, the field they created, provided an opportunity for his written works to be reprinted and reintroduced to a new generation of scholars, the Oyate, and American public audiences.

The Oceti Sakowin and other Indigenous communities are now defining their own literary traditions, moving away from a portrayal of the Oyate as mere victims of racism and moving toward their agency as resilient contributors to the world's achievements. From a turbulent past of racist settler colonialism, the literature of the Oyate is providing the optimism for societal change in the pursuit of a more hopeful future, which is to achieve a humane society on the shared earth of Dakota makoce. The literary works of Ohiyesa are now taking their rightful place as a part of forging that vision. As a writer Ohiyesa makes available in this book a means to discover ancestral voices from the Dakota oral tradition that have not been heard before. This narrative promotes understanding of another culture and adds to the richness of the varied human experience. The need to create is intrinsic to human nature, and the freedom to do so is a measure of a civil society that protects human rights. The literary work of Ohiyesa is a vital testament to the resilience and determination of the human spirit and the power of artistic expression.

Charles Alexander Eastman, Ohiyesa.

This Is Our Truth

KATE BEANE

I have attempted to paint the religious life of the typical
American Indian as it was before he knew the white man.
I have long wished to do this, because I cannot find that it
has ever been seriously, adequately, and sincerely done. The
religion of the Indian is the last thing about him that the man
of another race will ever understand.

OHIYESA (CHARLES ALEXANDER EASTMAN)
The Soul of the Indian, 1911

SOME OF THE FONDEST MEMORIES I HAVE AS A NATIVE GIRL
growing up in the 1980s are of singing Dakota hymns at Christ-
mas service with my grandmother at the First Presbyterian
Church in Flandreau, South Dakota. This place—built in 1873
and the oldest regularly attended church in the state of South
Dakota—is significant both as a space for worship and as a lasting historical monument in remembrance of our more recent
twentieth-century Reservation Era community and family

story. Many of our relatives are buried in the cemetery adjacent to the church: foundational leaders of our community like Jacob and John Eastman, who were father and older brother to Ohiyesa (Charles), and their descendants through my grandparents. Though they had been converted to Christianity, these relatives were brought up knowing and living by our Dakota wicohan, or way of life, and despite what many may believe, they never lost the fundamental teachings and belief systems of who we are as Dakota people. No matter how hard those who sought to change us tried to destroy our enduring spiritual connections, these practices and teachings live on in our communities today.

The church is one place of Christian Dakota worship. But as significant as our community churches are to our history and spiritual faith, there is a much larger and older place of worship that we as Dakota people honor and revere. I always knew that the natural world that surrounds and nourishes us is our true house of prayer and connection to the spirit world and to Tunkasida, or God. This is a world that makes sense amidst the chaos that we struggle through today. And yet, these teachings, though held tightly and remembered by a few, are not as well known today within our family as the more recent teachings of the Christian faith. The reasons for this lapse in remembrance and generational sharing have to do with our history as people who were impacted by colonialism and displaced by war. As Grandfather Ohiyesa writes in his introduction to this book, "the efforts of the government and the missionaries, . . . in order to civilize quickly, have succeeded in silencing their teachers and all Indianism." This purposeful silencing has had devastating impacts on our families and communities, and yet we remember. These teachings have been preserved by brave knowledge keepers, such as what is written here. These teachings relate the power and sacredness of Kunsi Maka (Grandmother Earth) and all that she provides for us as human beings that has been practiced, retained, and respected over thousands of years. These teachings reach further back than any building structure or practice of worship, and we are here and continuing to thrive as a people because of them.

Charles Alexander Eastman, one of the earliest residents of the Flandreau Isanti (Santee) Dakota community, has a strong legacy to be remembered and honored in his ancestral and childhood home of Mni Sota, Canada, and South Dakota, as well as the places he lived as an adult, most specifically areas of New England along the East Coast and Washington, DC. His books continue to be widely shared throughout the world. Ohiyesa was one of the first American Indian physicians, one of the earliest environmentalists, and a fearless American Indian rights advocate. He is remembered by many as a visionary and leader for his people. But to us as relatives, he is also a community documentarian and family storyteller. We are forever grateful for the words he typed into the eternal record in such detail, so that we might continue to know our origins and traditions as proud Dakota people today. The stories he recounts here are those that he heard growing up amidst our own people. They were told while we lived in our own territories, during a time of which we can only dream, before we were removed from our Mni Sota homelands by the US government in 1863.

As Gwen Westerman and Bruce White relate in *Mni Sota Makoce: The Land of the Dakota*, "The Dakota people are called Wicaŋhpi Oyate, Star people. Our spirits came from the creator down the Canku Wanaǧi, the 'spirit road,' more commonly known as the Milky Way."[1] The Dakota—the eastern group of the Oceti Sakowin (Seven Council Fires)—are comprised of the Bdewakantunwan, Wahpekute, Sisitunwan, and Wahpetunwan tribal bands, which are then broken up into even smaller tiospaye, or extended family units that historically camped together according to seasonal migration patterns.

Since time immemorial, Dakota people have lived in the Mni Sota region. "The Land Where the Waters Reflect the Sky" is how we translate this name of Mni Sota, which represents the cast that the sky shines on the many waters that cover this landscape, and it is thus also translated as "Land of Sky Blue Waters" or "Cloudy Waters." The literal meaning can change with each season. This is expressive of the true beauty of our language as visually descriptive of this place we have always called home.

There is more than one site of Dakota creation in Mni Sota. Two sites are widely considered to be the most prominently known places of origin: Bdote (Where the Rivers Meet) in the Twin Cities area, below where Fort Snelling stands today, and Bde Wakan (Spirit or Sacred Lake), which is now most commonly known as Mille Lacs, located one hundred miles north of the metro area. I was taught that different bands have their own stories, and that as Indigenous peoples we were put onto the earth in more than one place because each is the location we are tasked with protecting and stewarding. The origin story in the legend Ohiyesa recounts is not centralized in a specific location; it teaches of our beginnings, wherever they may be.

Many of us in Mni Sota Makoce with a vested interest in the writings of our grandfather Ohiyesa have longed to know what happened to his original manuscripts, wondering if any of his papers had survived over time. As Dakota relatives, we often speculate about what was edited in or out (likely by his wife, Elaine) to make his work more approachable to a larger and whiter audience, for mass publication. When we reconnected with our relatives in the East, we found the answer: his descendants there had curated his papers carefully. His writings hold the traditions and memories of our ancestors going back to the beginning of time.

These are oral histories for the generations of today. The stories are delivered as if spoken to the reader-listener, and there is tremendous value in this personal voice that comes directly from our ancestors. While it is certainly preferable to hear an elder tell these stories, we do not always have this opportunity; publication is another way to retain this information and this intimate voice for future generations. I purposefully treat this manuscript as *history*, and not *legends*, as oftentimes the latter term has been used to minimize the very real and powerful nature of our ways and beliefs. This is our truth.

This recounting of our creation is not a record of the location we come from as a people. It contains teachings about how we came to be created, and it explores the dynamics of how we formed our relationships with one another here on earth, as family members made up of humans, animals relatives, land, and the universe. Ohiyesa knew that time was of the essence in capturing these stories. He first wrote them down, in Dakota, in 1885. Five years later, he committed to confirming the twelve lessons with Weyuha, one of only three men then capable of repeating the full legend. Within the heart of each of the stories are teachings and lessons to be learned, as is usually the case in our tradition. And the way in which the stories are told, as if we are sitting with Weyuha around the fire, and with instructions on how the story is to be told to our wakanyeza (children), then recounted by them in their own voices to be retold to the next generation—this is a true treasure to behold. The instructions that we receive in how to pass down this information is both healing and comforting to read, as it inspires me to know that these teachings have continued and will continue on within our communities.

Included within these writings are stories of Unktomi, the sneaky trickster, whose many exploits have been well documented by many Native storytellers, and his rival Eayah. Though renditions of a select number of these tellings can be found in some form or another in other publications by Eastman, none are told in such detail and order as we have here, marking this collection as distinct and unique.[2] The sequence in which these stories unfold is particularly compelling. The teachings build upon one another in a manner that follows proper protocol and cultural integrity, so they can be passed down and taught to younger generations appropriately.

Each of these stories has its own life span among our peoples, and some are told more than others. Unique variations of the stories shared here (and in other of Ohiyesa's published works) have also been documented or passed down orally by relatives of other communities from various tribal bands of Dakota, Nakota, and Lakota peoples. Some stories are better known today than perhaps they were in previous generations that did not have the same freedoms to share them as we do now. The boarding school era and other impacts of colonialism have certainly diminished the widespread knowledge of these narratives. Stories such as "Stone Boy," a particular favorite in my home, and published by Ohiyesa in other texts, has different and yet very similar variations told among our communities by those who continue to hold these teachings. Regardless of the variation, the fundamental lessons of the stories remain the same, and the fact that these stories traveled throughout our many tiospaye speak to their resilience, to the wide breadth of storytelling connections, and to their importance among our people.[3]

These stories have been lightly edited for typographic errors, punctuation, and other minor issues by Charles Eastman's great-granddaughter Gail Johnsen. The story and heart of the writer's words are here, with very little polishing—this book does not include the "flowery" poetic flow of the previously published works that were edited by Ohiyesa's wife, Elaine Goodale Eastman. I have always appreciated the respect that Grandfather Ohiyesa showed toward the women in our family, and I find comforting the great care for these words and legacy that women in our family have shown in keeping these stories safe. As Grandfather writes, it was women who first came into being in this world: "She came through Nature; he came direct from the Spirit, therefore he has the seed. She came in this manner so that she may give the body to the Spirit."

I do believe that our Grandfather Ohiyesa would be happy to know that his tiwahe is sharing these words with the world today. He would be even happier to know that his people are still holding strong to these stories, that we are still learning and sharing these teachings of worldly strength and human weaknesses, of both the tragedy and humor that we experience in living, and that we continue to seek to hold deeper knowledge about this world we all live in together. Grandfather Ohiyesa, I commit to you that we will continue to share this knowledge with our children for generations to come. Nina wopida tanka, Unkanna (with much gratitude, Grandfather).

Contributors

DR. KATE BEANE (Flandreau Santee Sioux Dakota and Muscogee Creek) is the great-great-granddaughter of Charles Alexander Eastman's brother John. She holds a BA in American
Indian Studies and a PhD in American Studies at the University
of Minnesota, Twin Cities. She served as a Charles A. Eastman
Pre-doctoral Fellow at Dartmouth College and as a President's
Postdoctoral Fellow at the University of California, Santa Cruz.
She led the Native American Initiatives department at the Minnesota Historical Society until 2021, when she became the executive director of the Minnesota Museum of American Art. She
is adjunct faculty in American Indian Studies at the University
of Minnesota; she serves on the boards of Vision Maker Media
and the Lower Phalen Creek Project; and she was appointed by
Governor Tim Walz to serve on the Capitol Area Architectural
and Planning Board in St. Paul. She and her family worked to
restore the Dakota name Bde Maka Ska to Lake Calhoun, in
her ancestral homeland of Bde Ota (Minneapolis). She believes
that the dominant narrative of history should be updated to

honor the languages, lives, and legacies of its Indigenous peoples and that public spaces and museums should be welcoming and comfortable places for us all.

SYDNEY D. (SYD) BEANE (Flandreau Santee Sioux) is the great-grandson of Charles Alexander Eastman's brother John. Born in 1942 on the Mdewakanton Dakota/Flandreau Santee Sioux Reservation in South Dakota, he is a professional educator, social worker, documentary filmmaker, and community organizer. He has bachelor of arts and master of social work degrees, and he taught at Arizona State University, San Francisco State University, and Minneapolis Community and Technical College and at a Minnesota high school. He reorganized and administered American Indian Centers in Phoenix, Arizona, and Lincoln, Nebraska, and he was cohost for eight years of *21st Century Native American*, a talk show carried by ABC-TV. He is a founder of the Native Media & Technology Network (NMTN), which recruited and trained American Indian youth for employment opportunities in the entertainment industry. He was a national board member of the Center for Community Change and served as western regional director in San Francisco. He served on the boards of Native American Public Telecommunications (Lincoln, Nebraska), Native Public Media (Oakland, California), and MIGIZI Communications (Minneapolis). He was the coproducer, writer, and director of *Native Nations: Standing Together for Civil Rights*, a documentary on the American Indian Civil Rights Movement released by ABC, NBC, and the Hallmark Channel. He is the executive producer of *Ohiyesa: The Soul of an Indian*. Syd and his wife, Becky (Muscogee Creek), currently reside in Plymouth, Minnesota.

GAIL JOHNSEN is the great-granddaughter of Charles and Elaine Eastman. In the early 1970s she finished graduate school with a PhD in linguistics and decided that her next years would most valuably be spent in caring for her growing family and helping her husband in his work. As their children matured, she returned to education as a language teacher for a number of years. Language and, by extension, culture have always interested her. In retirement, she has had a chance to broaden those interests and make new connections through work on family history, in addition to expanding her efforts in several areas of volunteer services to her community.

GABRIELLE WYNDE TATEYUSKANSKAN is the great-great-granddaughter of Charles Alexander Eastman's brother David. She is a visual artist, writer, and poet who lives in the rural community of Enemy Swim on the Lake Traverse Reservation in South Dakota. She is a longtime member of the Oak Lake Writers' Society. Her work has been published in *American Indian Quarterly*; Waziyatawin Angela Wilson, *In the Footsteps of Our Ancestors: The Dakota Commemorative Marches of the 21st Century*; Oak Lake Writers' Society, *This Stretch of the River*; Oak Lake Writers' Society, *He Sapa Woihanble: Black Hills Dream*; John E. Miller, *What Makes a South Dakotan*; and *Yellow Medicine Review*. She is one of six people profiled in Diane Wilson's *Beloved Child: A Dakota Way of Life*.

YVONNE WYNDE is the great-granddaughter of Charles Alexander Eastman's brother David. She attended all of the types of education systems offered to Native American children: country day schools, mission schools, federal boarding school, and public schools. She graduated from St. Mary's School at Springfield,

South Dakota, and with honors from the University of Minnesota. She received a master's in education from Harvard University and returned for a certificate of advanced study. She was the first member of the Sisseton Wahpeton Sioux Tribe to earn a degree from Harvard; she is now the oldest living woman veteran at the Sisseton Wahpeton Lake Traverse Reservation. She raised four children and now has twelve grandchildren and twelve great-grandchildren.

Yvonne served on the committee that wrote the federal Tribally Controlled Colleges Assistance Act of 1978 and its associated regulations. She served at several tribal colleges in the Dakotas and Nebraska in administrative positions, as a faculty member, and as a counselor; she served as an officer for the American Indian Higher Education Consortium. She was inducted into the South Dakota Hall of Fame in 2004. In all her work, Yvonne has sought to instill the importance of the Dakota language, history, culture, and arts among young adults.

A Note on Editing
the Dakota Legend of Creation

CHARLES ALEXANDER EASTMAN WORKED WITH EDITORS ON
the many books he published. He knew that the draft for this
book would be copyedited, and he would not have wanted
typos, dropped words, and other errors to appear in print. In
making minor editorial revisions in this text, we have attempted
to change only obvious errors and matters of syntax that diminish clarity.

We followed the edits Eastman made to the typescript. His
daughter Dora made further edits that we have not followed,
except when they correct the same minor errors we have found.
We have addressed many matters of punctuation, added para-
graph breaks (especially in passages of dialogue), and added
occasional line breaks. We left his occasional mixed verb tenses
unedited. We have generally retained Eastman's capitalization;
where capitalization was inconsistent, we revised it to reflect
what he used more often. The inconsistent capitalization of
"spirit" proved particularly challenging, and we retained his

usage except for one case in which he was clearly referring to Eshnaicage. We have capitalized references to the Legend.

In about forty instances, without using brackets or otherwise flagging the change, we restored words that had been dropped; almost all were pronouns, articles, prepositions, conjunctions, and forms of "to be." We moved five misplaced phrases or sentences.

To help readers navigate, we added titles to the numbered chapters. In the original typescript, Eastman called his introduction a foreword.

Eastman's spellings of Dakota names reflect what was used at the time, and they often guide pronunciation. We removed hyphens between syllables and words, and we made spellings consistent; we also deleted pronunciations he sometimes added parenthetically. Eastman uses a few Lakota spellings, which we left unchanged, as they suggest the fluidity of the language and his use of it. He and his publishers did not use Dakota orthography or diacritical marks in his other books.

Eastman used the phrasings and spellings of his time. We have left unchanged some phrasings that carry and evoke stereotypes: princess (daughter of a leader), chief (leader), Medicine man (healer), warrior (soldier), and the like. We have also retained his spellings of Dakota words and names that are now spelled differently: for example, how (hau), teepee (tipi), ene-teepee (inipi), tonka (tanka), Unktomi (Inktomi), Eshnaicage (Isna Icage), Eayah (Iya), and Unktehe (Unktehi).

Dakota spellings and orthographies vary among speakers and communities. We have kept the spellings provided by the authors of the essays in this book, choosing not to impose uniform treatment.

Notes

Notes to "A Journey through Time and Family"

1. For examples, see "The Bride of an Indian," *New York Times*, June 19, 1918; untitled article, *Richmond Times*, June 20, 1918.

2. Charles Alexander Eastman, *From the Deep Woods to Civilization* (Boston: Little, Brown and Company, 1916), 2–3.

3. Elaine Goodale Eastman to Rose Dayton, [undated] 1936, Sophia Smith Collection of Women's History, Smith College Archives, Northampton, MA. Both Charles and Elaine followed the usage of the time in referring to "Indians."

4. Elaine Goodale Eastman, Foreword to *From the Deep Woods to Civilization*, vi.

5. Eleanor Mensel to Raymond Wilson, August 19, 1975, handwritten copy in author's possession.

6. Marybeth Lorbiecki, in an unpublished manuscript (copy in author's possession), referenced a donation of "the remainder of his [Charles's] unfinished works and research" by Elaine to the Friends of the Middle Border Museum in Mitchell, South Dakota. According to Lorbiecki's information, that museum later suffered a fire in which it was assumed both the writings and the records were destroyed.

7. Charles Eastman to H. M. Hitchcock, January 14, 1935, in H. M. Hitchcock papers, Edward E. Ayer Collection, Newberry Library, Chicago.

8. Elaine Goodale Eastman to Rose Dayton, undated [winter, 1936?] and February 3, 1937, Sophia Smith Collection of Women's History, Smith College Archives.

Notes to "Ohiyesa: From the Sacred Earth of the Oceti Sakowin, a Literary Tradition"

1. Charles Eastman to H. M. Hitchcock, January 14, 1935, in H. M. Hitchcock papers, Edward E. Ayer Collection, Newberry Library, Chicago.

2. Anne Dilenschneider, "An Invitation to Restorative Justice: The Canton Asylum for Insane Indians," *Northern Plains Ethics Journal* (2013): 105–8; David E. Walker, "'A Living Burial': Inside the Hiawatha Asylum for Insane Indians," *Indian Country Today*, November 9, 2015; and Laura Waterman Wittstock, "Native American Gulag: The Hiawatha Asylum Cemetery," *Indian Country Today*, February 3, 2016.

Notes to "This Is Our Truth"

1. Gwen Westerman and Bruce White, *Mni Sota Makoce: The Land of the Dakota* (St. Paul: Minnesota Historical Society Press, 2012), 18.

2. See, for example, Charles Alexander Eastman, *The Soul of the Indian* (Boston: Houghton Mifflin, 1911), 119–45; Charles Alexander Eastman, *Wigwam Evenings* (Boston: Little, Brown and Company, 1928), 109–15, 125–46.

3. The story of Stone Boy appears in Charles Alexander Eastman, *Indian Boyhood* (New York: McClure, 1902), 126–37.

Index

In the Beginning, the Sun:
The Dakota Legend of Creation
was designed and typeset by Judy Gilats
in St. Paul, Minnesota. The text typeface is
Corundum Text and the display face is Agenda.